Roads Less Traveled
IN NORTHEAST OREGON

A Guide to Back Roads and Special Places

Steve Arndt

About the Roads Less Traveled Series:

"The series will stitch together the state's history and habitat for anyone who pays as much attention to what they're driving through as where they're going." — Bill Monroe, *The Oregonian*

www.roadslesstraveledoregon.com

Also by Steve Arndt:

Roads Less Traveled in North-Central Oregon
Roads Less Traveled in Northwest Oregon I
Roads Less Traveled in Northwest Oregon II
Roads Less Traveled in South-Central Oregon
Roads Less Traveled in Southeast Oregon
Roads Less Traveled in Southwest Oregon

Roads Less Traveled in Northeast Oregon
A Guide to Back Roads and Special Places

Steve Arndt

Copyright © 2010 Steve Arndt
All rights reserved.

Photographs by
Diane Arndt of Woodburn, Oregon

Maps by
Justin Eslinger, Box Lunch Design

Printed in the United States of America

ISBN: 978-0-9844294-0-0

Front Cover:
 Sheep Rock in the John Day Fossil Beds National Monument
 (Photograph by Diane Arndt)

Back Cover (from top to bottom)
 Ranch entrance between Seneca and Canyon City
 Barn in Prairie City
 Sumpter Valley Railroad Engine in Sumpter
 Old schoolhouse near Island City
 Dirt road and mountains near Cornucopia
 (Photographs by Diane Arndt)

Designed by

Justin Eslinger | Box Lunch Design
boxlunchdesign@gmail.com

Dedicated to my granddaughter

Audrey Christine Arndt

To darling baby Audrey, who already gobbles up books like there will never be another meal, and who shrieks with delight at every page turn: we hope you'll love this book, and even more, love exploring "roads less traveled" with us. May you grow to appreciate Oregon's beauty and history as much as we do and help keep it in trust for those who follow.

I shall be telling this with a sigh
Somewhere ages and ages hence:
Two roads diverged in a wood, and I—
I took the one less traveled by,
And that has made all the difference.

—Robert Frost (1874-1963)
from his poem, "The Road Not Taken"

Acknowledgements

Diane Arndt	Photographer, proofreader, partner
Justin Eslinger	Box Lunch Design
Inland Empire Store	Adams
Dyann Swanson and the Athena Café	Athena
Visitors Information and Baker City Chamber of Commerce	Baker City
The Cove Library	Cove
The Old Mercantile and City Hall	Dayville
Echo Restaurant and Bar and City Hall	Echo
The Haines Mercantile	Haines
The Stockman Bar and the Pine Valley Museum	Halfway
Helix General Store	Helix
Frank Harkenrider, former mayor	Hermiston
David and Lee Manuel	Hot Lake
The Imbler Market and local residents who freely shared information about their community	Imbler
Grant County Chamber of Commerce	John Day
John Day Visitors Center	John Day
Chamber of Commerce and Visitor's Information Center	La Grande
Dave Cherry	Lostine
The Meacham Store	Meacham
The granddaughter of Dunham Wright	Medical Springs
Poe the Raven and his owners	Middle Bridge
Boyer's Grocery Store	Monument
Mt. Vernon City Hall	Mt. Vernon
The Cunningham Sheep Company	Nolin
Information Center and Chamber of Commerce	Pendleton
Annie of Anne's Restaurant and Fred Mitchell	Pilot Rock
The owners of the Pondosa General Store	Pondosa
The Prairie City Pharmacy and Linda Harrington of the Strawberry Mt. Inn Bed and Breakfast	Prairie City
The Elephants Trunk and the City Hall	Stanfield
Greater Sumpter Chamber of Commerce	Sumpter
The Union Hotel and Another Place in Time Bed and Breakfast	Union
Enterprise and Joseph Visitors Center	Wallowa Country
The Wallowa History Center and local resident Mark Highberger	Wallowa
Michelle Ashley and the Long Branch Cafe	Weston
Bob Gilliland	Weston

Contents

Foreword	i

Pioneers, POW's and Peas — 1
Stanfield to Pendleton (91 miles)

Stanfield	3
Hermiston	4
Holdman	6
Helix	7
Umapine	9
Milton-Freewater	10
Athena	12
Adams	14
Pendleton	16

Meander Along the Emigrant Trail — 19
Meacham to Tollgate (68 miles)

Meacham	21
Deadman Pass Rest Area	22
Mission	23
Cayuse	24
Thorn Hollow	25
Weston	26
Tollgate	28

Pioneer Echoes, Pilot Rocks and Hot Springs — 29
Rieth to Ritter (156 miles)

Rieth	31
Nolin	32
Echo	33
Lena	36
Vinson	37
Pilot Rock	38
Ukiah	40
Dale	41
Ritter	42

Gold, Chinese Medicine and Metasequoia — 43
Prairie City to Dayville (221 miles)

Prairie City	45
Seneca	47
Canyon City	48
John Day	49
Mt. Vernon	51
Long Creek	53
Monument	55
Kimberly	56
Dayville	58

Gold, Ghost Towns, and Granite — 59
The Baker City Loop (166 miles)

Baker City	61
Haines	64
Granite	66
Sumpter	68
Whitney	69
Austin	70
Austin Junction	71
Unity	72
Hereford	73

From the Geographic Center of the US to a Horn of Plenty — 75
North Powder to Cornucopia (89 miles)

North Powder	77
Telocaset	78
Medical Springs	79
Pondosa	80
Keating	81
Middle Bridge	82
Sparta	83
New Bridge	84
Richland	85
Pine	86
Halfway	87
Cornucopia	89

From the Grande Ronde Valley to the Wallowa Mountains — 91
La Grande to Imnaha (141 miles)

La Grande	93
Hot Lake	95
Union	96
Cove	98
Island City	99
Alicel	101
Imbler	102
Summerville	103
Elgin	104
Wallowa	106
Lostine	109
Flora	112
Enterprise	113
Joseph	115
Imnaha	118

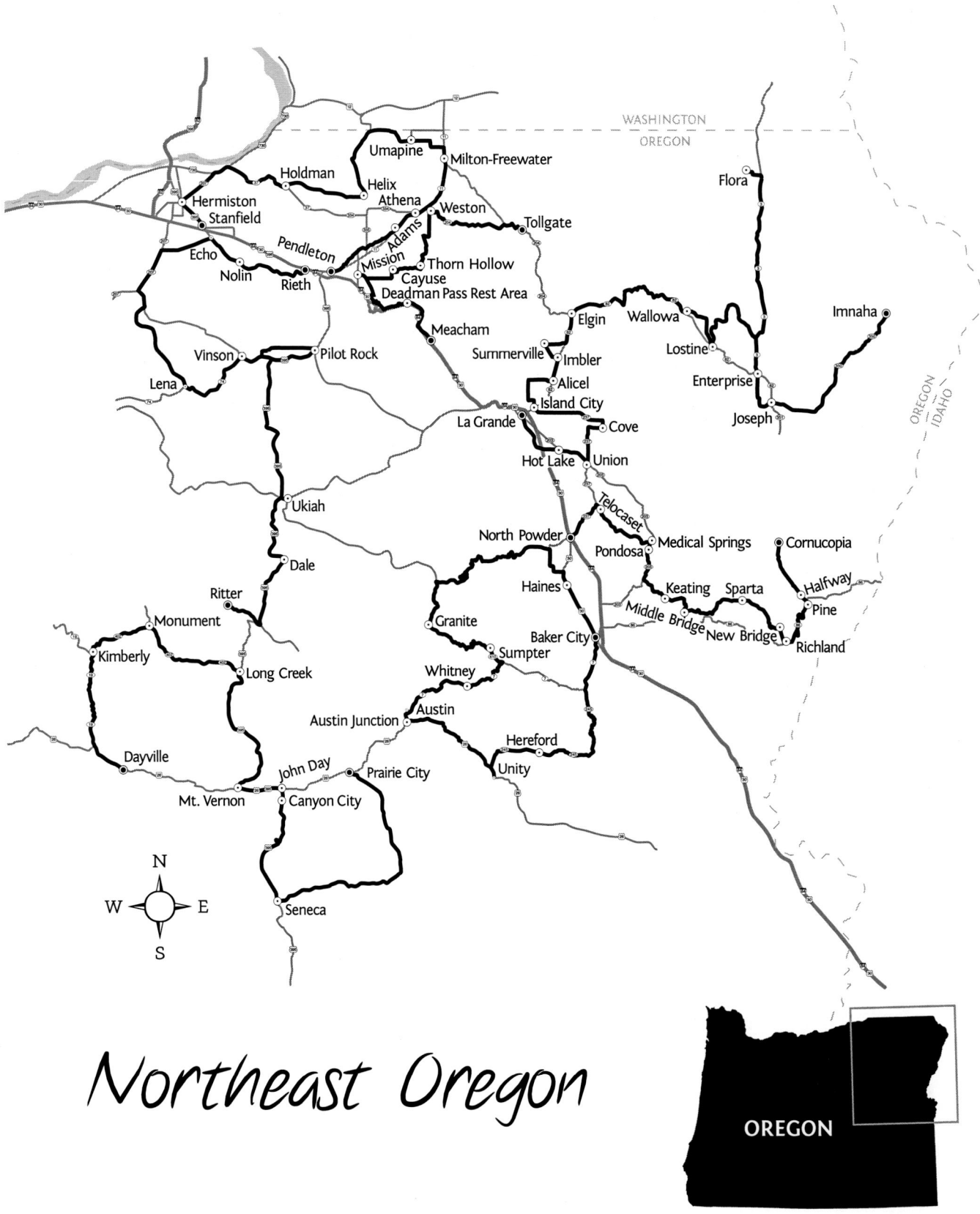

Northeast Oregon

Foreword

You don't simply drive through this treasure of a state we call Oregon.

You savor it. You drink its beauty, relish its diversity, honor its history.

And the diet isn't complete without the best lessons you can find.

Having made a career myself of traveling across the state on the way to and from news stories and features for *The Oregonian*, the pages of my *Oregon Geographic Names* are well-worn from constant referral.

But they don't tell nearly everything and some places I pass, no, MANY places I pass, simply aren't in there.

Enter Steve Arndt of Woodburn. Arndt is an educator, professionally and, now, literarily with *Roads Less Traveled in Northeast Oregon*, the fifth book in a series he's doing about rural roads across the state and how they stitch together habitat and lesser highways for those who pay as much attention to what they're driving through as where they're going.

The guides focus on short loops of 50 to 150 miles off beaten freeway paths, which in northeast Oregon opens a wide, wide panorama of pavement for Arndt's keen sense of place and history. He's picked some of the best in an area of Oregon often called "Little Switzerland."

Pick up any of his guides of roads close to your home and take just one trip for a sip of Steve's keen sense of place, history and perspective.

You'll be hooked, as I am.

Savoring the others, one day at a time.

—Bill Monroe, *The Oregonian*

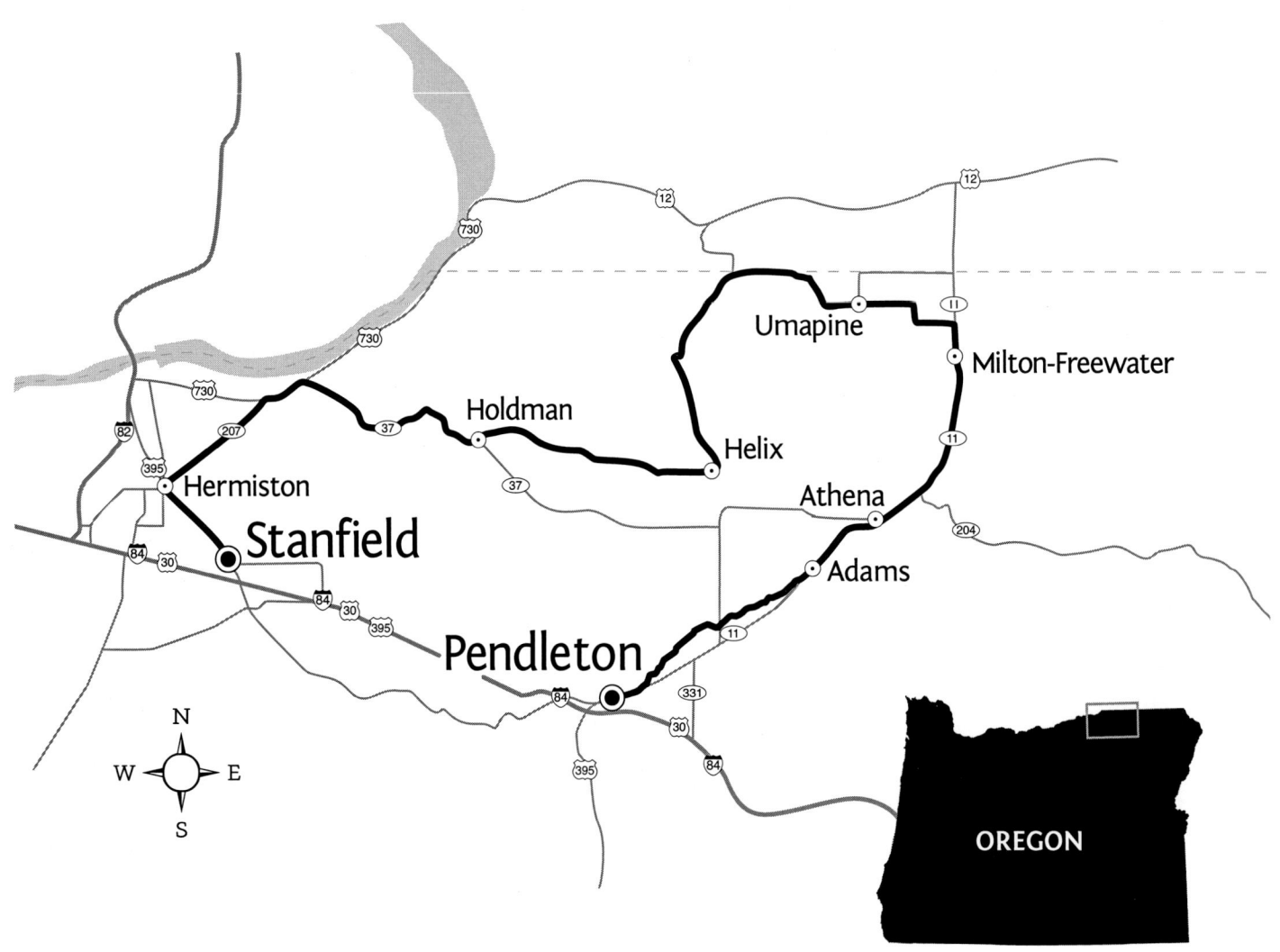

Stanfield to Pendleton

Stanfield 3
Hermiston 4
Holdman 6
Helix 7
Umapine 9
Milton-Freewater 10
Athena 12
Adams 14
Pendleton 16

Pioneers, POW's and Peas

Stanfield to Pendleton (91 miles)

Miles of fertile farmland that produce famed peas and watermelon connect small, agricultural communities along the route from Stanfield to Pendleton.

Stanfield, easily accessed from I-84, exit 188, was originally a stop on the old Pendleton to The Dalles stage route. During World War II, sleepy Stanfield housed German POWs and frequently showcased bandleader Doc Severinsen and The Arlington Blue Notes in the historic dance hall. From Stanfield, the route continues to Hermiston, a community that grew rapidly when the Umatilla Army Depot opened in the 1940s.

Near the Columbia River, just outside Hermiston is a naturally occurring geologic formation named Hat Rock by Lewis and Clark as they progressed westward toward the Pacific in 1804. Between Holdman and Umapine, the route follows along the Oregon-Washington border, and then continues to Milton Freewater, once known as the Pea Capitol of the West. Following stops in Athena and Adams, the route ends in Pendleton, home to the annual Pendleton Round-up and the historic 1812 camp of the Astoria-bound Wilson-Hunt Price party.

the rolling hills and fields near Milton-Freewater

Stanfield

Elevation: 492 feet

Location:
45.46.838 N • 119.13.063 W

Services:
gas, food, lodging, RV, B&B

The railroad came through this settlement in 1881 and the post office opened under the name of Foster in 1883. In 1907, the name Foster was changed to Stanfield for US Senator Robert N. Stanfield, who owned much property in the area, and who, along with his brother, owned one of the largest sheep ranching operations in North America. Stanfield continued to grow and was platted in 1908 and incorporated in 1910. As irrigation for crops became available, farming replaced sheep ranching in economic importance. According to Frank Harkenrider, former mayor of Hermiston who grew up in Stanfield, German POWs were interned here during World War II. Harkenrider says that Stanfield was the only mainland US city bombed during the war when a bomb fell off of a US plane during maneuvers, destroying a tavern located at the corner of Main and Furnish. Stagecoach Road, north of town, follows the old route of the Stanfield-Pendleton Stage Line.

a local watering hole

the Old Stanfield School which now hosts a church

Points of Interest

- **Stanfield Mercantile and Grocery** *(105 S. Main)*
  The store and upstairs dancehall opened in 1904 as the Stanfield Millinery Shop. Doc Severinsen and the Arlington Blue Notes often played here in the 1940s.

- **Stanfield City Hall** *(155 S. Main)*
  Originally built as a drugstore, the city hall is also the business location of Ramona's Gourmet Kitchen food products, which specializes in making pepper jelly. Displayed on the wall is a 1925 picture of Senator Stanfield.

- **Stanfield Bank** *(Main and Coe)*
  Constructed in 1905 with leaded glass windows.

- **Beauty Shop** *(Main Street)*
  Built as the Stanfield Hardware Store and Tonsorial Parlor, it later housed an indoor shooting gallery before conversion to a beauty shop.

- **Columbia Land Company** *(120 Coe - next to the old Stanfield Bank)*
  The original home of the Century Land Speculation Company that tried to glamorize local real estate, selling land at inflated prices. Gargoyles adorn the roof of this building.

- **Stanfield Hotel** *(Coe and Main)*
  Opened in 1905.

- **Old Stanfield School** *(Coe and Wayne)*
  The 1914 school was later used as a church.

- **Stanfield Grange #657** *(225 Sherman)*
  Built near railroad tracks.

- **Old House** *(225 S. Main)*
  One of Stanfield's oldest private residences.

- **Stanfield Park** *(Coe and Sherman)*
  Playground, restrooms, horseshoe pits, BBQ, and covered picnic area.

- **Early Auto Dealership** *(615 Coe)*
  Former auto sales and service.

- **Foster Cemetery** *(on Foster Cemetery Road, one mile south of town)*
  Dates to 1861.

- **Hermiston Cemetery** *(one mile south of town near the railroad tracks off of the Umatilla-Stanfield Highway)*
  Dates to the 1880s.

- **Pleasant View Cemetery** *(Edwards Road and Stanfield Canal Road, two miles NE of downtown)*
  Opened in 1913.

Stanfield to Hermiston

Distance:
2.2 miles

Directions:
Go north on Highway 395, the Umatilla-Stanfield Highway.

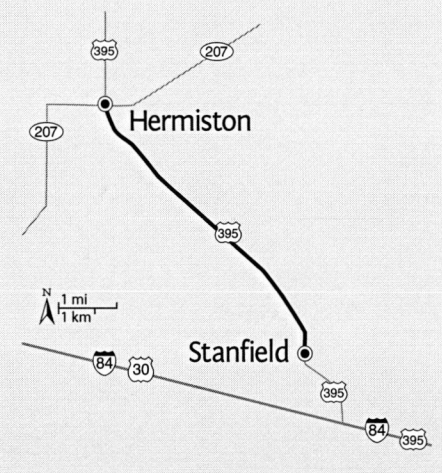

Points En Route

(mileage from the intersection of Main and Harding near the bridge)

0.4 miles:
Stanfield School complex.

1.8 miles:
OSU Extension Service Experimental Farm.

2.2 miles:
Hermiston

Hermiston

Elevation: 476 feet

Location:
45.50.281 N • 119.17.309 W

Services:
gas, food, lodging, RV

In the 1860s and 1870s Hermiston was called Six-mile House and featured an old west bar and hotel. The railroad came through town in 1903, the post office opened in 1905, and the city incorporated in 1907. The wife of Colonel J.F. McNaught suggested the name Hermiston when she read

RoeMark's Department Store

the name in Robert Louis Stevenson's novel, *The Weir of Hermiston*. Only a few of Hermiston's original buildings remain today. It was not until the 1940s, when the Umatilla Army Depot opened, that Hermiston began to grow. Hermiston is nicknamed the "Community of Parks" because it has a dozen dedicated parks and playgrounds within the city limits. Hermiston is the watermelon capitol of Oregon and is also known for desert honey and potatoes. The largest employers in Hermiston are J.R. Simplot, Lamb-Weston Frozen Foods (frozen french fries), Hermiston Frozen Foods and Marlette Industries, builder of manufactured homes.

Points of Interest

- **Hermiston Cemetery**
  (Port Drive)
  Dates to the early 1900s.

- **Bank of Hermiston**
  (101 E. Main)
  Built in 1907.

- **First National Bank**
  (106 E. Main)
  Opened in 1907.

- **Pheasant Café**
  (149 E. Main)
  A restaurant since 1907.

- **Cozy Corner Tavern**
  (198 E. Main)
  The 100-year-old bar was relocated from Idaho City in 1944. Concrete blocks used in construction were manufactured in Echo and Stanfield.

- **RoeMark's Department Store**
  (201 E. Main)
  Built in 1907. Originally the Hermiston Tavern and Independent Order of Odd Fellows Hall.

Hermiston to Holdman

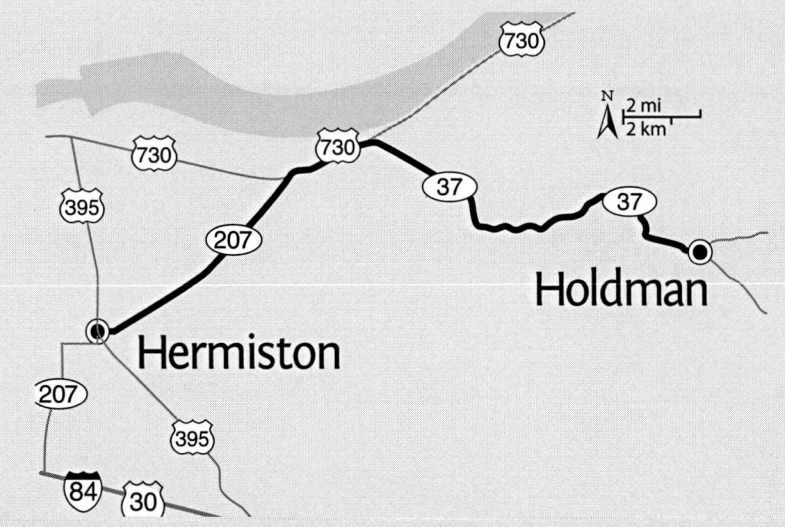

Distance:
21.3 miles

Directions:
Drive east on Main Street (Highway 207)

Points En Route

(mileage from the corner of Highway 395 and Highway 207 - 1st and Main)

3.0 miles:
Columbia Grange #307. Built in the 1920s.

3.5 miles:
Cold Springs Reservoir and Wildlife National Refuge. The 3000-acre refuge was established in 1909 and is one of the oldest in the United States.

6.3 miles:
Cattle ranch. The cows have white stripes around their midsections.

7.1 miles:
Intersection of Highway 207 and Highway 730. Turn right onto Highway 730, heading east.

7.8 miles:
Hat Rock State Park. This geographic feature, identified by Lewis and Clark, is the first discernable land formation mentioned by the explorers as they traveled down the Columbia. Picnicking, swimming, restrooms, fishing, and boat launch. No overnight accommodations and no admission fee.

8.6 miles:
Panoramic views of the Columbia.

9.0 miles:
(to the right on Highway 37, the Pendleton-Cold Springs Highway) Site of the former community of Cold Springs, an important boat landing for ships carrying wheat. The community died when the railroad made the boat landing unnecessary. Cold Springs boasted a school, several homes, a railroad section house and a farmer's warehouse. The post office opened in 1878 under the name of Arroyo, changing to Cold Springs in 1880. That office closed in 1883. A water canal from Cold Springs Reservoir to Hermiston was completed in 1918, providing irrigation to farmers.

9.2 miles:
The elevation increases as the road winds through layers of basalt.

14.9 miles:
South Fork of Cold Springs River.

15.3 miles:
Old ranch with outbuildings.

16.7 miles:
Cold Springs Ranch.

21.3 miles:
Holdman

Holdman School

Holdman

Elevation: 775 feet

Location:
45.53.026 N • 118.56.062 W

Services: none

This small, unincorporated community was named after two brothers that settled here in the late 1800s. The Holdman post office opened in 1900 and the Holdman School first held classes in 1922. The cemetery, on the hill above the grain elevators, dates to 1905.

Points of Interest

- **Holdman School**
  School District #105. Opened in 1922.

- **Wooden Grain Elevator**
  Built in the early 1900s. The elevator is identified PGG, for Pendleton Grain Growers. An old windmill stands nearby.

- **Holdman Farms**
  The original 1882 Holdman farmhouse.

Wooden grain elevator

Holdman to Helix

Distance: 14.0 miles

Directions:
Turn left onto Holdman Road, and drive east.

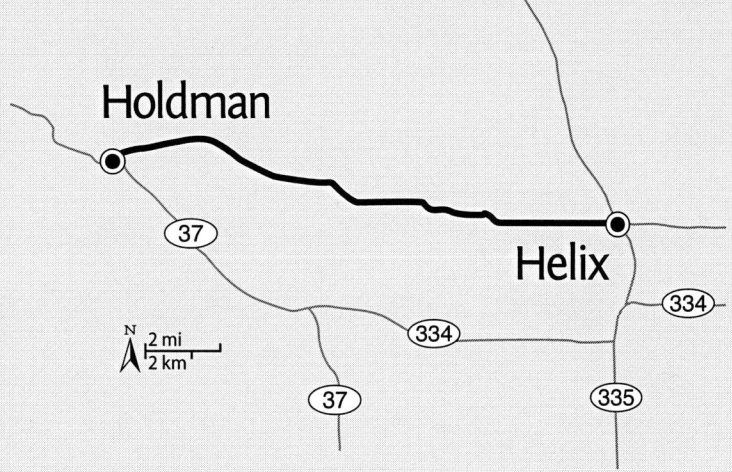

Points En Route

(mileage from the intersection of Holdman Road and Highway 37)

0.3 miles:
An old farmhouse stands near the Middle Fork of the Cold Springs River.

3.1 miles:
Several outbuildings and an old farmhouse.

3.7 miles:
An old farm with weather vanes, grain elevator and outbuildings.

4.0 miles:
Brown Family Century Farm, 1886.

5.6 miles:
Windmill and farmhouse.

7.5 miles:
Site of the former community of King's Corner. Local wheat farmers built the large grain elevator.

7.8 miles:
100 plus year-old farm.

10.0 miles:
The site of Ruth's Corner, named for the wife of an early settler. An abandoned farmhouse and outbuildings are all that remain.

11.0 miles:
A wooden grain elevator, an old farmhouse, outbuildings and windmill.

14.0 miles
Helix

Helix

Elevation: 1698 feet

Location:
45.51.200 N • 118.39.468 W

Services: gas, food

Helix was originally called Oxford in 1880, the same year the post office opened. The name Oxford was changed to Helix in 1908 when a long time resident had a painful ear infection in the 'helix' of the ear. Today, Helix is an important wheat growing and shipping center.

the historic Helix Hospital

Points of Interest

- **Helix Hospital**
  (Main and Arthur)
  The original clinic and infirmary building is now a private residence.

- **Masonic Lodge**
  (Main and Concord)
  Built in 1889.

- **Helix Hardware** (205 Concord)
  Turn of the century construction.

- **Post Office** (209 Concord)
  This newer post office replaced the old one that was located in the general store.

- **Old Livery Stable** (212 Solar)
  The stable was remodeled and converted into a private residence.

- **Helix Bank**
  (Cleveland and Concord)
  Built in the early 1900s.

- **Old House** (313 Cleveland)
  A large, two-story.

- **Old House** (115 Main)
  One of the older houses in Helix.

- **Griswold High School**
  (120 Main)
  The school district dates to 1889.

- **Old Service Station**
  (Columbia and Main)
  Once a full service station, now abandoned.

- **Helix City Hall** (119 Columbia)
  Occupies the old elementary school building.

- **Helix General Store and Tavern** (206 Columbia)
  Built in 1920 and displays many old photos.

- **Old House** (306 Vesper)
  Victorian architecture.

- **Helix Rodeo Grounds**
  Home of the annual Memorial Week-end Rodeo.

- **Helix City Park**
  Swimming pool, picnic area, restrooms, BBQ, and playground.

- **Helix Cemetery**
  Dates to 1882.

Helix City Hall

Helix to Umapine

Distance: 20.9 miles

Directions: From Harrison and Columbia, go north on Harrison, which becomes Vansycle Road. This travel segment includes 6.5 miles of well-maintained graveled roads. To avoid the gravel, follow the road signs to Milton-Freewater.

Points En Route

(mileage from the corner of Harrison and Columbia)

1.6 miles:
An old farmhouse and outbuildings.

1.9 miles:
Hutchinson-Kern Century Farm (80974 Vansycle Road). The outbuildings have cupolas.

2.4 miles:
Old fruit trees surround an abandoned farmhouse.

3.6 miles:
Wind generators in the distance.

4.9 miles:
Former community of Stanton. Only a few trees, the HR&R Ranch and a PGG grain elevator remain.

6.5 miles:
Turn right onto Butler Grade Road. Pavement turns to gravel at this point.

6.8 miles:
Old farmhouse with stained glass windows (82900 Butler Grade Road).

7.1 miles:
Excellent view of wind generators.

8.3 miles:
A radio tower and fantastic view of the valley.

12.6 miles:
Intersection. Stay on Butler Grade Road.

13.0 miles:
Pavement returns at the intersection of Butler Grade Road and Umapine-State Line Road. Turn right onto Umapine-State Line Road, which exactly follows the Oregon-Washington border.

14.4 miles:
An old school house converted to a residence.

18.0 miles:
Two old farmhouses with outbuildings.

20.0 miles:
Quarter horse ranch.

20.9 miles:
Umapine

the road between Helix and Umapine

8

Umapine

Elevation: 658 feet

Location:
45.58.577 N • 118.29.808 W

Services: food

Originally called Vincent (thus the inscription on the school building), the name was changed to Umapine when it was discovered that there was already a community named Vincent in Wallowa County. Umapine was the name of a famous Umatilla (Cayuse) Indian Chief. The Umapine post office opened in 1916 and closed in 1966. On July 15, 1936 a magnitude 5.7 earthquake struck Umapine, causing much damage and changing the flow of ground water. Umapine is an important wheat-growing center and is known for its fruit, peas, beans, alfalfa, horses and cattle.

Umapine (Vincent) School

Points of Interest

- **Umapine Mercantile Store**
  Open since 1907.

- **Old School Bronze Foundry**
  (84678 Ringer Road)
  Occasionally open for tours.

- **Umapine Community Center**
  Formerly the Umapine Baptist Church.

- **Umapine (Vincent) School**
  (Umapine Road and Ringer)
  Built in 1911.

- **Umapine Church**
  (Umapine Road and Ringer)
  Built about the same time as the school.

Umapine to Milton-Freewater

Distance:
6.2 miles

Directions:
From the store, drive east on Ringer Road.

Points En Route

(mileage from the Umapine store)

2.7 miles:
An 1876 Century Farm.

3.9 miles:
The Hudson Bay irrigation canal.

4.4 miles:
Reese Orchards, since 1925.

5.4 miles:
Former community of Fruitvale. The Pribes Station and Store still stand.

6.1 miles:
Lefore Orchards.

6.2 miles:
Milton-Freewater

Milton-Freewater

Elevation: 1021 feet

Location:
45.56.606 N • 118.23.741 W

Services:
gas, food, lodging, RV, B&B

Milton and Freewater were settled as separate communities. Milton, the older of the two, was located on the old stage line between Wallula, Washington and La Grande, Oregon. It was settled in 1867 as a dry town and prohibited the sale of alcoholic beverages. The post office opened in 1873 and was named by the first postmaster, W. A. Cowl, who came from Milton, New York. The town was platted and became a municipality in 1886. In 1889, J.B. Mahana, who owned the local water rights, established the community of New Walla Walla. Mahana gave free water to anyone who would settle in his newly created town, and the name was appropriately changed in 1890 to Freewater. The residents of Freewater could buy, consume, and manufacture alcohol as long as it was in 'one gallon measure,' because federal law restricted the sale of lesser amounts. The two communities joined in 1951 and the Milton-Freewater post office officially opened. The two communities have been important agricultural centers. In the 1940s, the first three-story gravity flow pea cannery was established here and operated for over thirty years. As late as the 1960s, Milton-Freewater was the world's biggest producer of peas. At one time, Milton-Freewater was home to three colleges: Milton Academy (1886), Columbia College (1900), and Columbia Junior College (1908). Many old and historic homes are located in the Milton and Freewater communities.

First Christian Church

Points of Interest

- **Yantis Park**
  (DeHaven and SW 2nd)
  Athletic Fields, aquatic park, picnic.

- **Train Depot** *(3rd and Main)*
  Built in 1926, now the Milton-Freewater Senior Center.

- **First Christian Church**
  (5th and Main)
  An imposing structure.

- **Bank of Milton-Freewater**
  (6th and Main)
  Opened in 1906.

- **First National Bank**
  (6th and Main)
  Built in 1906.

- **Milton-Freewater City Hall**
  (7th and Main)
  Formerly Columbia College, converted to its current use in 1910.

- **Oregon Trail Heritage Marker**
  (near City Hall)
  Before the Whitman Massacre, the Oregon Trail went through Milton-Freewater.

- **Valley Christian Center**
  (8th and Main)
  Old and very large.

Train Depot

Milton-Freewater

Points of Interest (continued)

- **Opera House** *(8th and Main)*
  The former 1909 Alooff and Talbert Building.

- **Freewater Park**
  (off 8th and Main)
  The oldest park in Milton-Freewater has a picnic area and playground. The land for the park was designated in 1890.

- **Knights of Pythias**
  (10th and Main)
  Dates to 1909.

- **McLoughlin High School**
  (Main Street)
  Named after Hudson Bay's John McLoughlin. Opened in 1915.

- **Grace Presbyterian Church**
  (Main)
  Turn of the century construction.

- **Milton Masonic Lodge #96**
  (210 SW 2nd)
  An ornate building that dates to 1909.

- **Old Warehouse** *(4th and Robbins)*
  Located near the railroad tracks.

- **Old Houses** *(108 and 158 NW 5th, 103 Robbins, 411 Evans)*
  An iron fence surrounds one of these beautiful homes.

- **Freewater School**
  (8th and Evans)
  The Chronology of Schools states that the school was built in 1915. Today it houses grades 3, 4 and 5.

- **Old City Cemetery**
  (go west on 8th Avenue)
  This small, private cemetery also dates to 1878.

- **Old Houses** *(at the intersections of 12th, 13th, and 14th, with Chestnut, Walnut, and Mill)*
  Several examples of beautiful, ornate, 100-year old homes.

- **Frazier Farmstead Museum**
  (1403 Chestnut Street)
  A beautifully maintained 1868 farmhouse and barn. Closed in January, February and March and open on Thursdays, Fridays and Saturdays.

- **IOOF Cemetery**
  (Milton Cemetery Road)
  Dates to 1878.

Old warehouse

Freewater School

Milton-Freewater to Athena

Distance:
9.9 miles

Directions:
From Main and 14th, turn right, and drive south toward Athena.

Points En Route

(mileage from the corner of Main and 14th) Main Street becomes Highway 11.

1.3 miles:
Milton-Freewater Water Tower.

4.0 miles:
Deep ravine and farmhouse.

6.7 miles:
Weston Junction. Continue on Highway 11 toward Athena.

9.5 miles:
Turn right on Wild Horse Road.

9.8 miles:
Beautiful Victorian house.

9.9 miles:
Athena

Athena

Elevation: 1701 feet

Location:
45.40.702 N • 118.29.490 W

Services: gas, food

In 1866, New Yorker Darwin Richards homesteaded 2000 acres on Wild Horse Road. Richards operated a stagecoach stop and post office, which was known as Richard's Station. This stage station was located about half way between Walla Walla and Pendleton. A community grew around the stage stop and, due to its location, was named Centerville. Unfortunately, this was the same name as a community in Washington, so the original four-block settlement was re-named Belleview. That name did not hold and the community went through several more name changes, including Squawtown, Yellow Dog and Mud Flats. The Centerville post office opened in 1878 and officially changed to Athena in 1889, named after the most important goddess in Greek mythology. The first church was built in 1873, the first blacksmith shop in 1878 and the Baptist Church, which is now a Catholic Church, in 1890. The mortuary opened in 1890 and doubled as the furniture store. When the mortuary building was vacated, the new owners found three unused coffins in an upstairs room. Hodoka Motorcycles were sold and distributed in Athena from 1967-1979, but ceased operation when importing ended. The local newspaper, *The Centervillian*, ran from 1879 to 1985. Main Street once had two railroad depots, three saloons, and three doctor offices. An epidemic of diphtheria hit the community in 1878, and many souls were lost to the dreaded disease. The town incorporated in 1904. Many large, fancy houses were built with carriage entrances, turnarounds and detached garages. At one time, Athena was a major producer of peas. Every July, since 1899, Athena celebrates the Caledonian Games, a tribute to the community's New Caledonia (Scottish) roots. The games are held at the city park.

Old Ford Garage and Service Station

Points of Interest

- **Skate Park** (1st and Main)
  Newly constructed for local teens.

- **Ford Garage** (2nd and Main)
  Sales and service began in the late 1910s.

- **Masonic Lodge** (216 Main)
  The 1900 lodge building is now the home of International Harvester Farm equipment.

- **Hotel St. Nichols** (260 Main)
  Built by John Froome in 1880, now an apartment building.

- **Dudley House** (3rd and Main)
  Built in 1899 for Eugene Dudley. Dudley Road is named for this early settler.

- **City Hall** (306 Main)
  Previously a café.

- **Athena Drug Store** (312 Main)
  Continually operating as a pharmacy since it opened in 1906.

- **City Park** (3rd and Park)
  Established in 1878.

- **First National Bank** (352 Main)
  The bank opened in 1890, became the US Bank in 1939, and currently houses an antique store. The bank was robbed in the 1940s when robbers tunneled through a wall and stole $10,000 worth of coins. The hole in the concrete is still visible.

- **Old Gas Station** (4th and Main)
  Converted to a snack shop.

- **Post Office** (4th and Main)
  1904. Once housed the IOOF Lodge.

Athena

Points of Interest (continued)

- **Athena School**
  The 1897 school burned in 1975. The new school opened in 1977.

- **Blacksmith Shop**
  Now the Shell Station and Garage.

- **Underkirk House** (310 Washington)
  One of Athena's finest.

- **Fisher House** (415 Van Buren)
  Built in 1916.

- **Logsden House** (425 Van Buren)
  Built in 1909.

- **Christian Church Parsonage** (434 Van Buren)
  Dates to 1903.

- **Christian Church** (458 Van Buren)
  Opened in 1902.

- **Athena Christian Church** (Van Buren and 5th)
  Built in the early 1900s.

- **Kirk House** (528 Van Buren)
  The garage in the back of this 1900 home was once a stable.

- **Minnie Lively House** (345 5th)
  A stable was also built behind this house.

- **Wilson House** (324 High)
  Built in 1887 for Elizabeth Wilson.

- **J.R. King House** (424 High)
  Built in 1885.

- **Hugh Worthington House** (434 High)
  Built in 1900.

- **Jessie Legrove House** (533 High)
  Built in 1903.

- **James Nels House** (534 High)
  Built in 1892.

- **Dale Preston House** (553 High)
  There is a stable behind the house.

- **Miller House** (554 High)
  Built in 1893.

- **Athena Cemetery** (west of town at Sherman and Princeton)
  Dates to 1873.

St. Nichols Hotel

Athena to Adams

Distance:
4.8 miles

Directions:
From Main and 3rd, drive toward Highway 11.

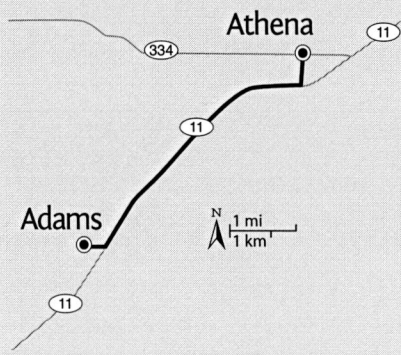

Points En Route

(mileage from the intersection at Main and 3rd).

0.4 miles:
Turn right on Highway 11, head west and south toward Pendleton.

1.2 miles:
Quarter horse ranch.

2.1 miles:
Old barns, rows of poplars and a farmhouse.

4.7 miles:
Turn right onto Spring Hollow Road toward Adams.

4.8 miles:
Adams

Adams

Elevation: 1624 feet

Location:
45.46.121 N • 118.68.757 W

Services: gas, food

Adams, a small community about thirteen miles northeast of Pendleton, was named for John F. Adams, an early wheat rancher and homesteader in the area. The post office opened in 1883, the same year the Walla Walla Railroad came through town. The community was platted in 1883 and established in 1893. The livery stable stood at the corner of Hale and Prescott. Adams was a very important wheat producer and shipping location. The community of Adams has fewer than 300 residents.

Adams School

Points of Interest

- **Adams Meat Company** (*across the railroad tracks on North Main*)
  Opened in the early 1900s.

- **Adams School**
  (*S. Main and Commercial*)
  The large school, built about 1911, is now a private residence.

- **Adams Store and Inland Mercantile** (*130 S. Main*)
  Built in 1885 and still in use. The building was made of bricks manufactured at the local Adams Brickyard, which supplied bricks for the city hall and the K. Wilkes residence at 280 Morrison. The café was added to the store in the early 1900s and serves breakfast and lunch. A few antiques and old photos are displayed in the store.

- **Ladies Club** (*160 S. Main*)
  Next to the city hall.

- **City Hall** (*190 S. Main*)
  The library and former IOOF building.

- **City Park** (*S Main and Wade*)
  Swings, picnic area, restrooms, tennis courts and playground.

- **Methodist Church**
  Built in 1884.

- **Episcopal Church**
  Opened in 1884.

- **Baptist Church**
  The first services were held in 1886.

- **Adams Saloon**
  Open since 1889. Originally located at the corner of Hale and Center.

- **Old House** (*280 Preston*)
  A large Victorian.

- **Old House** (*145 College*)
  One of the oldest residences in Adams.

- **Adams Cemetery** (*corner of Sherman and Pinkerton*)
  0.6 miles south of town off Sherman.

Adams Store and Inland Mercantile

Adams to Pendleton

Distance:
11.6 miles

Directions:
Go south on the Athena-Holdman Highway.

Points En Route

*(mileage from College and Preston)
Drive south on College, which becomes Wildhorse Road, toward Pendleton. There are frequent sections of gravel.*

0.3 miles:
"El Rancho Not So Grande" farm.

0.6 miles:
Pavement ends.

0.7 miles:
Pavement returns.

1.2 miles:
Pavement ends.

1.4 miles:
Pavement returns.

3.6 miles:
Large farm with grain elevators, outbuildings and an old farmhouse.

3.9 miles:
Old farmhouse with a carriage porch.

5.3 miles.
Stop. Cross the Havanna-Helix Highway, stay on Wildhorse Road toward Pendleton. Road improves.

6.9 miles:
Old farmhouse in the trees near the creek bed.

7.2 miles:
Road meanders through the creek-carved canyon.

8.1 miles:
Intersection with Myrick Road. Stay on Wildhorse Road.

9.0 miles:
Narrow bridge.

9.1 miles:
Round barn.

9.5 miles:
Former community of Fulton.

10.4 miles:
Deserted farmhouse.

11.6 miles:
Pendleton

round barn along the road to Pendleton

Pendleton

Elevation: 1200 feet

Location:
45.40.132 N • 118.47.531 W

Services:
gas, food, lodging, RV, B&B

Members of the Wilson-Price Hunt Party camped here in 1812. In 1860, Abram Miller first settled in the Pendleton area. In the 1864 election, Oregon delegates supported, as their choice for vice-president, Ohio political leader and democrat George Hunt Pendleton. Even though he did not win the nomination, he left an impression on area voters who named the newly platted city and county seat in his honor. In 1865, the post office opened under the name of Marshall, which was changed to Pendleton in 1869. Pendleton incorporated in 1880. The Pendleton Round-Up, an annual rodeo event, began in 1910, and is the largest four-day event of its kind in the United States. Pendleton was known as the "Entertainment Capital of Eastern Oregon" because it once had eighteen brothels and thirty-two bars in a four-block downtown radius. In the 1920s and 1930s, the KKK had a strong presence in Pendleton. Clan members wore white robes during the Round-Up Parades. In 1942, training for Lieutenant Colonel James "Jimmy" Doolittle's famous WWII raid on Tokyo was conducted at Pendleton Airfield. Grand, old houses in the North Main Neighborhood offer a wide representation of different architectural styles including Colonial Revival, Queen Ann, Mediterranean, Dutch Colonial, Tudor, Transitional, Greek Revival, Victorian, Gothic, Italianate and Craftsman Bungalow.

Rogers House along Main Street

Points of Interest:

- **Bowman Hotel** *(17 SW Frazer)*
  Built in 1905, now an office building.

- **Heritage Station Museum** *(108 SW Frazier)*
  This former railroad depot was constructed in 1910. It is adjacent to the old one-room Byrd Schoolhouse.

- **Empire Block** *(21-37 SW Emigrant)*
  The entire block was built in 1907 in the Italianate Style. The second floor was a brothel and hotel, and the Hop Sing laundry operated in the basement.

- **Pendleton Underground** *(34 SW Emigrant)*
  Walk through the underground tunnels that were home to businesses, hundreds of Chinese workers, and ladies of the night.

- **Post Office** *(105 SW Dorion)*
  Built in 1916 to replace the 1869 office.

- **Frazer Building** *(147 N Main)*
  Opened in 1881 as the Alexander and Frazer Store.

Heritage Station Museum

Pendleton

Points of Interest (continued)

- **Carnegie Building** (214 N Main) Built in 1916, the original library is now the Pendleton Center for the Arts.

First Christian Church

- **First Christian Church** (215 N Main) Beautiful stained glass windows adorn this 1908 church that replaced the one lost to fire. The stone was quarried in Baker County.

- **Rogers House** (311 N Main) This 7000 sq. foot Mediterranean Revival mansion was built in 1917 for a wealthy cannery owner. The house is open for tours and operates as a B&B.

- **Brock House** (320 N Main) 1904 Dutch Colonial with five bathrooms, nine bedrooms and a Palladian window. Built for the owner of Taylor Hardware.

- **Bowman Building** (6 S Main) Built in 1905 to resemble a castle.

- **Club Cigar** (138 S Main) One of the first saloons in town and built in two phases, the first in 1884 and the second in 1889.

- **Milarky Building 2** (203 S Main) Opened in 1883 and used as a drug store for 96 years.

- **Milarky Building 1** (209 S Main) Example of 1880s Italianate Commercial construction. The first brick building in Pendleton.

- **Columbia Hotel** (322-326 S Main) Built in 1900, the "modern" hotel boasted hot and cold running water, a café and electric lights.

- **LaFountaine Building** (332-338 S Main) Built in 1902. The first floor was a fancy restaurant and the second floor a hotel.

- **Children's Museum of Eastern Oregon** (400 S. Main) Interactive, hands-on exhibits.

- **Masonic Lodge** (403 S Main) Built in 1887 and later carefully restored. This was the first brick building south of Dorion.

- **Ferguson Building** (412-418 S Main) Built in 1903 as the "St. Helens Hotel."

- **Pendleton Chamber of Commerce** (501 S. Main) Helpful, friendly people will assist you.

- **Hamley Building** (28 SE Court) First opened in 1901 as a saddle and tack store.

- **Despain Building** (29 SE Court) An 1887 law office. The Knights of Columbus occupied the second floor.

- **LaDow Block** (210-239 SE Court) Opened in 1884 and completed in 1890. Included an opera house.

- **Pendleton Woolen Mills** (1307 SE Court) Begun in 1909, now open seven days a week.

- **Brown Building** (110 SW Court) Built as the Elks Lodge in 1919 and later converted to apartments.

- **Taylor-Brock Hardware** (220 SW 1st) Unique chimney flues adorn this 1886 building.

- **Fell House** (319 NE 1st) Built in 1899 and burned to the ground before occupancy. The symmetrical Colonial Revival with leaded glass windows was rebuilt the same year.

- **Oak Hotel** (327 SE 1st) The 1904 building opened as a hotel and later was a brothel.

- **Old Pendleton Firehouse** (225 SE 2nd) The first fire hall in town.

Livermore House

17

Pendleton

Points of Interest (continued)

- **Episcopal Church** *(241 SE 2nd)*
  Founded in 1872, this church was built in 1898. A Louis B. Tiffany stained glass window is part of its architecture.

- **Methodist Church** *(346 SE 2nd)*
  This "newer" church was built in 1906 so that the church members would not have to attend services next to a brewery. The old church, located on 3rd Street, was built in 1875, well before the brewery became its unwanted neighbor.

- **Col. Raley House** *(233 SE 4th)*
  Built in 1878 and since remodeled with additions.

One-room Byrd Schoolhouse

- **Clock Tower**
  (corner of SE 4th and Court)
  Over 100 years old.

- **Sommerville House**
  (104 SE 5th)
  Built in 1899.

- **Tallman House** *(428 SE Byers)*
  An 1896 Queen Anne. Tallman was a local druggist.

- **Dr. Smith Residence**
  (520 SE Byers)
  His 1894 home and office.

- **The Temple House**
  (523 SE Byers)
  Built in 1900 for the "Wheat King." Mr. Temple harvested over 4000 acres of wheat on his ranch.

- **Sophie Byers House**
  (602 SE Byers)
  Temple built this house for his daughter, Sophie, in 1900. The addition came in 1910.

- **Jurgen Mumm House**
  (612 SE Byers)
  Mumm, another successful wheat rancher, built this home in 1903.

- **Belts House** *(708 SE Byers)*
  Belts, a successful sheep rancher, owned 3000 acres of ground where he raised over 6000 sheep. The architecture of the 1917 house represents the Arts and Crafts style.

- **Swineburn-Jones House**
  (714 SE Byers)
  Built around 1895 for Dr. Swineburn.

- **Judd House** *(3 NE Ellis)*
  1903 Transitional with Greek Revival.

- **Livermore House**
  (203 NW Ellis)
  Built in the 1890s, this Queen Anne Victorian was the home of Pendleton's first mayor.

- **McCormack House**
  (313 NW Ellis)
  A wealthy wheat farmer built this 1907 Colonial Revival.

- **Cole House** *(5 NE Despain)*
  A Colonial Revival/Queen Ann built 1904-1907 with twenty-eight rooms for Pendleton's first surgeon.

Cole House

- **Clark House** *(203 NW Despain)*
  A 1912 Craftsman Bungalow, with five bedrooms and four baths.

- **Pioneer Park** *(4th and Despain)*
  Formerly a cemetery, now a city park with a few remaining grave markers. Most graves were moved to Olney Cemetery in SW Pendleton.

- **Anderson House**
  (504 NW Despain)
  Built in 1886 as a small Italianate and enlarged and embellished in the Queen Ann style in 1900.

- **Jackson House**
  (505 NW Despain)
  The Embellished Gothic Farmhouse was built in 1900 for C.S. Jackson, owner of the East Oregonian Newspaper.

- **Tamastlikt Cultural Institute**
  (72789 Highway 331)
  Take I-84 exit 216 to this state of the art Cultural Center of the Umatilla, Cayuse and Walla Walla Tribes.

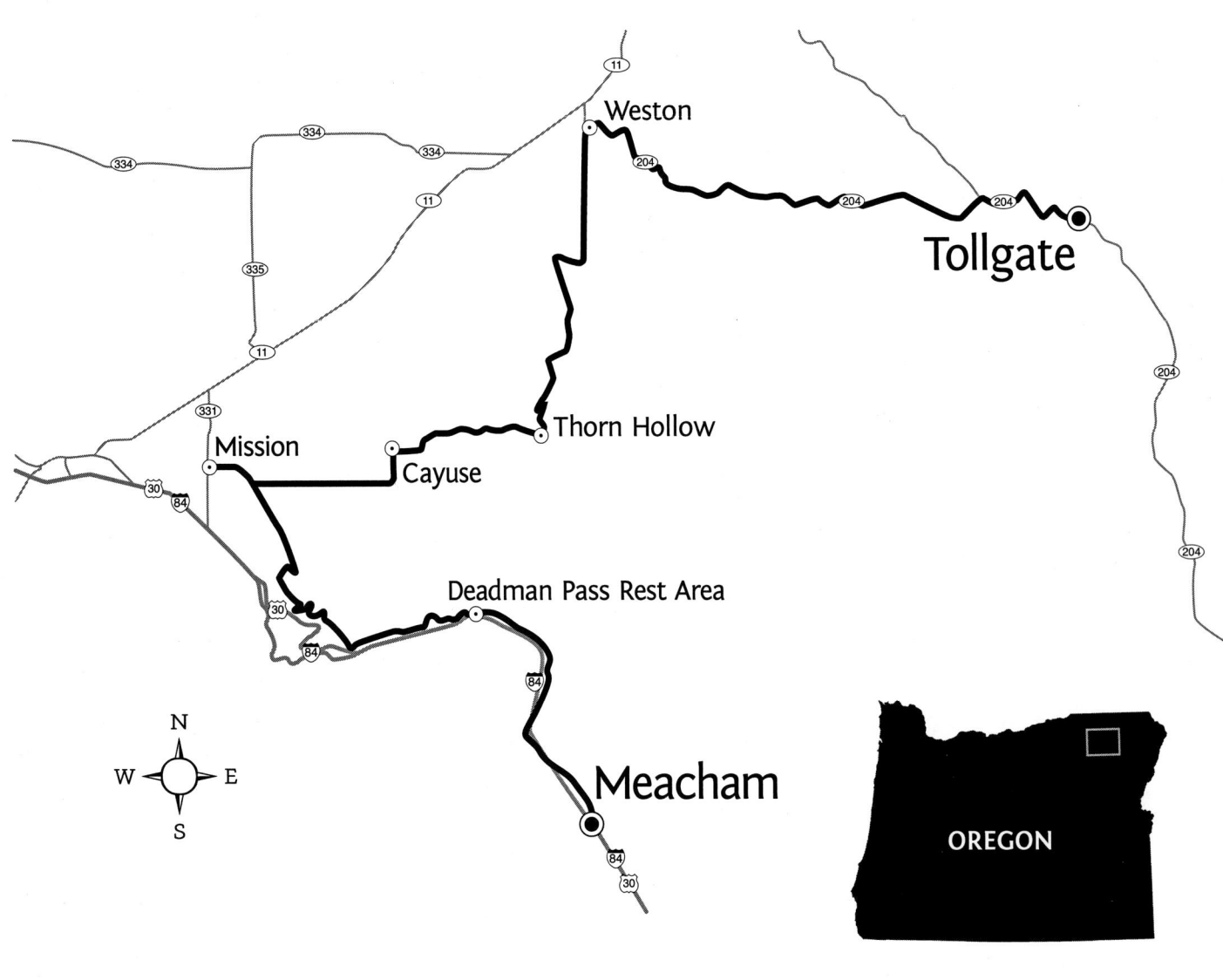

Meacham to Tollgate

Meacham 21
Deadman Pass
Rest Area 22
Mission 23
Cayuse 24
Thorn Hollow 25
Weston 26
Tollgate 28

Meander Along the Emigrant Trail
Meacham to Tollgate (68 miles)

The first leg of this route, Meacham to Mission, follows the old Emigrant Hill wagon road on the Oregon Trail. Thousands of pioneers encountered steep terrain, jagged rocks and dense, treed landscape as they crossed the Blue Mountains on this very road.

Since construction of I-84, which completely bypasses Meacham, this seldom used road affords breathtaking views of the Grand Ronde Valley as it winds toward Pendleton from the top of Cabbage Hill (Emigrant Hill). In the heart of the valley below is Mission, the 1855 headquarters of the Umatilla Indian Agency.

The route meanders northeast through the farmlands and forests of the Umatilla Reservation, through the communities of Cayuse and Weston, and ends in the mountainous, forested landscape at Tollgate.

the Blue Mountains as they fall towards Mission

20

Meacham

Elevation: 4055 feet

Location:
45.30.267 N • 118.25.333 W

Services: food

Meacham Store

In the 1840s, a stage station, known as Lee's Encampment, was established here, near the summit of the Blue Mountains. The name was changed to Meacham in the mid 1860s when brothers Alfred and Harvey Meacham operated and later owned the station. The station closed in the late 1870s and, in 1882, when the rail line came through, the name was changed to Encampment. For a short time in the late 1880s, Meacham was called Jerusalem. The name was changed back to Meacham in 1890. President Warren Harding gave a speech here in 1923. Although Meacham is typically cold and blanketed in snow during the winter months, the temperature dipped to an incredible -52°F in 1933.

Points of Interest

- **Meacham Hotel** (*68610 Main*)
  Built in 1903, the hotel is now a private residence. An old wagon and a log house are adjacent to the hotel, now called "Melody Mountain Camp."

- **Meacham Store**
  Open since 1885. Many old photos are displayed inside the store.

- **Rock Monument**
  Erected in 1935 by the Meacham Women's Club to commemorate those who died on the Oregon Trail.

- **Log Cabin House**
  Built near the old school.

Meacham to Deadman Pass Rest Area

Distance:
8.8 miles

Directions:
From the intersection of Main and Old Emigrant Hill Road (at the Oregon Trail Store), drive north on Old Emigrant Hill Road (aka: Old Highway 30) toward Pendleton.

Points En Route

(mileage from the store)

0.1 miles:
The 1914 Meacham School is located at the corner of College Street and Old Emigrant Hill Road.

2.1 miles:
Old Emigrant Hill Road parallels I-84.

3.0 miles:
Emigrant Springs State Park. A popular pioneer stop along the Oregon Trail. Camping, picnicking, trailer hook-ups, cabins, showers and historic displays.

3.9 miles:
Viewpoint.

5.3 miles:
Entering Umatilla County.

5.7 miles:
Scenic Viewpoint

8.8 miles:
Deadman Pass Rest Area. RV dump, restrooms, pet area, picnic areas, vending machines, information kiosk.

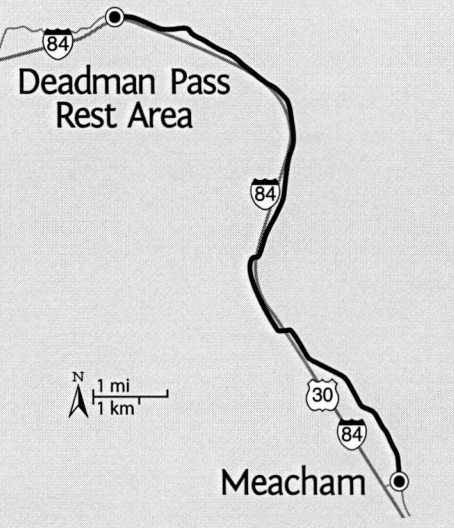

Deadman Pass Rest Area

Elevation: 3626 feet

Location:
45.35.910 N • 118.30.315 W

Services: RV dump

Deadman Pass is located on the old Oregon Trail. In 1878, four men were killed near here during the Bannock Indian War. Pioneers knew this treacherous pass through the Blue Mountains as Crawford Hill.

the changing vegetation

a view down Cabbage Hill

Deadman Pass Rest Area to Mission

Distance:
15.4 miles

Directions:
Go to the underpass and drive north on Old Highway 30 toward Deadman Pass Viewpoint.

Points En Route

(mileage from the underpass)

1.4 miles:
Radio towers.

2.7 miles:
Old fence.

4.2 miles:
Radio towers and satellite receivers.

4.5 miles:
View of the valley.

4.8 miles:
Intersection with Poverty Flat Road. Stay on Old Highway 30.

5.0 miles:
Change in vegetation.

5.5 miles:
A commanding view of the valley below and Pendleton in the distance.

6.1 miles:
More radio towers.

6.2 miles:
Scenic view.

7.6 miles:
Deciduous forest.

10.0 miles:
Home with private wind generator and solar panels.

11.1 miles:
Old farm with outbuildings.

13.7 miles:
Take Cayuse Road.

14.2 miles:
Yellow Hawk Tribal Center.

14.3 miles:
Nixyaayii Community School.

14.8 miles:
Old Tribal Headquarters building (located on "A" Street).

15.2 miles:
An old wagon and farm implements.

15.4 miles:
Mission

Mission

Elevation: 1233 feet

Location:
45.40.053 N • 118.41.009 W

Services: food

The Umatilla Indian Agency Headquarters was established in 1855 for the Cayuse, Walla Walla and Umatilla Tribes. Mission gets its name from the Roman Catholic and Presbyterian Missionaries that settled here to bring religion to the displaced Native Americans. The 1878 Headquarters building was burned during the Bannock Wars and later rebuilt.

Old Tribal Headquarters

Points of Interest

- **Wildhorse Gaming Casino** *(located on Mission South Road)* Follow signs to this popular tourist attraction.

- **Tamastslikt Cultural Institute and Museum** *(near the Casino on Mission South Road)* Interesting historic and cultural exhibits.

Mission to Cayuse

Distance:
7.4 miles

Directions:
From the intersection of Mission and Highway 131, travel east, backtracking toward Cayuse.

Points En Route

(mileage from the convenience store at the corner of Mission and Highway 131)

0.6 miles:
Confederated Way, housing for Umatilla Tribe members.

0.9 miles:
Ball fields.

1.2 miles:
Park, playground, and restrooms.

1.6 miles:
Turn left onto Cayuse Road.

4.5 miles:
Cayuse turns into River Road.

7.2 miles:
Turn left onto North Cayuse Road.

7.4 miles:
Crossing the Umatilla River.

7.4 miles:
Cayuse

Cayuse

Elevation: 1416 feet

Location:
45.40.565 N • 118.08.369 W

Services: none

Only fifty-nine people currently reside in this small community, named for the Cayuse Indians. The Cayuse Indians were a Waiilatpuan Tribe that lived near the headwaters of the Umatilla, Grand Ronde, and Walla Walla rivers, and between the Deschutes River and the Blue Mountains. The tribe was associated with the Nez Perce and the Walla Walla. There was a stage station and later a rail station at this location. The post office opened in 1867.

weathered outbuilding

Cayuse to Thorn Hollow

Distance:
5.5 miles

Directions:
From Cayuse, drive east on North Cayuse Road.

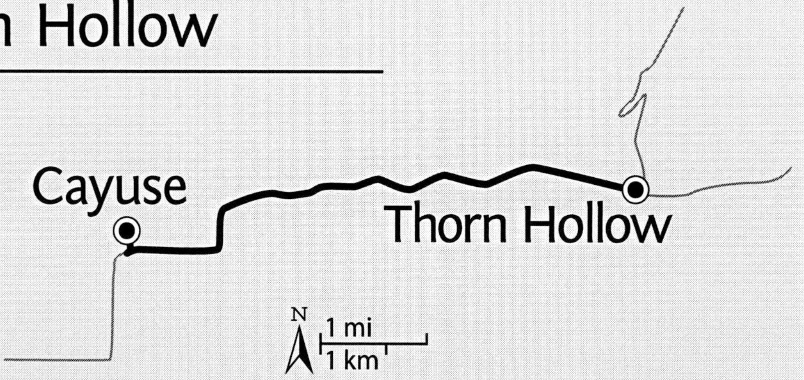

Points En Route

(mileage from the bridge)

0.1 miles:
Turn left onto Cayuse Road, a curvy, winding road.

2.3 miles:
Deciduous forest.

3.1 miles:
Three homes in a row. This is the site of Homly, named after the Chief of the Walla Walla Tribe. The Union Pacific Railroad had a station here in 1928.

4.1 miles:
Railroad tracks.

4.4 miles:
Old farm.

5.2 miles:
Old schoolhouse.

5.4 miles:
Cayuse Road becomes Thorn Hollow Road.

5.5 miles:
Thorn Hollow

Thorn Hollow

Elevation: 1604 feet

Location:
45.40.995 N • 118.27.584 W

Services: none

Thorn Hollow was an old rail stop, named for the thorn bushes that grow in abundance here. The community died when the Thorn Hollow Rail station closed. Remains of the community include a few homes near the river. The 1910 Red Elk Cemetery is 1.1 miles east on River Road.

Thorn Hollow School

Thorn Hollow to Weston

Distance:
11.9 miles, of which 2.6 miles is graveled.

Directions:
Return across the river and turn left onto Spring Hollow.

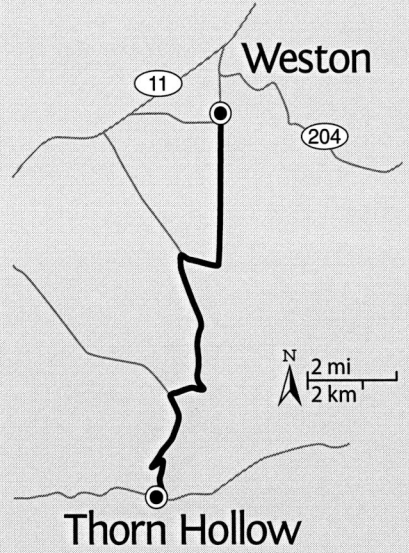

Points En Route

(mileage from the intersection of Thorn Hollow and Spring Hollow)

0.1 miles:
Fish Hatchery.

0.2 miles:
Crossing the Umatilla River.

2.8 miles:
Intersection with Duff Road. Stay on Thorn Hollow.

3.4 miles:
Turn right onto Eagle Creek Road.

3.4 miles:
Gravel begins.

4.3 miles:
Stay left on Eagle Creek Road.

5.3 miles:
Intersection with Hansel Road.

6.0 miles:
Old farmhouse. Pavement returns.

6.6 miles:
Old outbuildings.

7.7 miles:
Turn right onto Wildhorse Road.

8.8 miles:
Go straight on McClain Road.

11.2 miles:
Kees Cemetery Road. Also known as Blue Mountain Cemetery, the first burial was in 1875.

11.7 miles:
Farm with an old gas pump.

11.9 miles:
Weston

Weston

Elevation: 1812 feet

Location:
45.48.802 N • 118.25.507 W

Services: gas, food, B&B

Weston City Hall

This once-thriving community, first known as Mitchell's Station, was founded in 1865. The post office opened in 1867. After becoming postmaster in 1869, T.T. Lieuallen renamed the community Weston, after his hometown of Weston, Missouri. Prior to incorporation in 1878, a fire destroyed all but two businesses in July 1874. A second fire, in October 1883, destroyed many residences. Weston was home to a major brick making company that made most of the bricks used in construction of Eastern Oregon Normal School, now called Eastern Oregon State University. The home of prominent storeowner, Mr. Saleng, was also constructed with bricks from this plant and likely is the reason the house survived the destructive fires. In 1902, Weston had a population of over 800 residents, more than it has today. At that time, the community boasted a school, post office, doctor's clinic, city hall, brickyard, lumber mill, flourmill, train depot, two mercantiles, four saloons, five churches, and six banks. Weston is home to Conagra, a division of Smith Frozen Foods. Located in the Walla Walla Valley and situated at the foot of Weston Mountain, Weston is the second oldest town in Umatilla County after Pendelton.

Points of Interest

- **Saleng House** *(Poplar and Water)*
  Currently under restoration.

- **Kees House** *(Depot and Water)*
  The oldest house in Weston.

- **Old Houses** *(Bruce and Water)*
  Two of the older houses in Weston.

- **Weston Community Church** *(S Water)*
  The oldest church in town, dating to 1891.

- **Elliot Memorial Park** *(Main and Water)*
  Playground, picnic area, skate park and restroom.

- **Weston Train Depot** *(100 Main)*
  This 1895 building has been a saloon, grocery store, meat market, dry goods store and a candy shop. There are old photos inside.

along the drive between Thorn Hollow and Weston

Weston

Points of Interest (continued)

- **D and F Café** (102 E Main)
  Built in 1912 and always a café.

- **Jarman Department Store** (103 E Main)
  Constructed in 1895.

- **Weston Library** (104 E Main)
  Built in 1900.

- **Tavern** (105 E Main)
  Built in 1895. Now the Blue Mountain Inn.

Weston Schools

- **106 E Main**
  1895 construction, it housed the post office from 1910-1960.

- **107 E Main**
  Blue Mountain Valley Center. Built in 1895 as the Raynaud Building.

- **108 E Main**
  The City Library housed in a former residence.

- **Masonic Building** (109 E Main)
  The 2nd floor meeting place of the Masons is virtually intact since the building was constructed in 1895.

- **City Hall** (160 E Main)
  Originally a bank. A sign over the entrance reads, "Marshall, Weston, Oregon, 1865." Several photos of Weston at its peak are displayed inside.

- **Long Branch Café and Saloon** (201 E Main)
  The oldest commercial building in Weston and one of two that survived the fires. Built in 1874 as the Saleng and Reese Store. Historic items displayed here include a painting that shows the fountain as it stood at the downtown Main and Franklin intersection. The old fountain, found years later, was relocated to its current location at the corner of Main and Water.

- **Memorial Hall** (206 E Main)
  Built in 1895 as the Opera House and now home to the Senior Center. The building was moved to this location in 1918. Included in the Opera House are a gym, stage, and dance floor.

Weston's oldest buidling

- **United Methodist Church** (400 E Main)
  Built in 1906 as the Methodist-Episcopal Church.

- **Methodist Church Parsonage** (406 E Main)
  Circa 1909.

- **Old House** (Hill and Main)
  Two-story with a carriage porch.

- **Weston Schools** (District 8 and 11)
  Built in 1915 and enlarged in 1927. The entrance steps afford a panoramic view of the community below.

- **Weston Cemetery** (Main to Old Weston Cemetery Road)
  Dates to 1871. Located near Pine Creek.

house between Weston and Tollgate

Weston to Tollgate

Distance:
19.1 miles

Directions:
From the Saleng House, go north on Water.

Points En Route

(mileage from the Saleng House)

0.1 miles:
Turn right.

0.5 miles:
Stop sign. Turn right onto Highway 204. Follow signs to Tollgate.

0.9 miles:
Old farm and barn.

1.6 miles:
Great view.

5.3 miles:
Old farm.

6.2 miles:
Road narrows.

7.3 miles:
An older two-story house.

9.2 miles:
Electric substation.

9.7 miles:
Log cabin.

11.0 miles:
County Maintenance Yard.

11.4 miles:
More log cabins.

11.9 miles:
Meadow Wood Springs Speech Camp.

15.4 miles:
Blue Mountain Private Resort.

15.9 miles:
Lincton Mountain Restaurant.

17.3 miles:
WWB Academy Lodge.

18.6 miles:
E.J. Haynie Viewpoint.

19.1 miles:
Tollgate

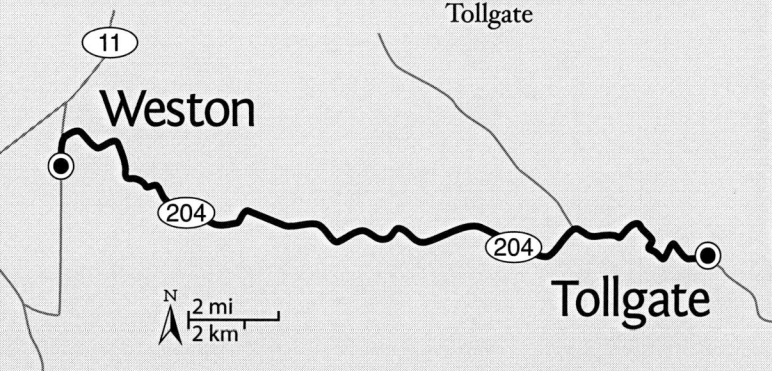

Tollgate

Elevation: 5052 feet

Location:
45.47.137 N • 118.06.556 W

Services: gas, food, B&B

Located in the Umatilla National Forest, Tollgate had an actual gate where pioneers and later travelers paid a fee to use the road that crossed the Blue Mountains. The first tolls were collected in the 1870s. The post office was not established until 1941 when the area became a popular place for hunting, fishing and winter recreation.

Points of Interest

- **Tollgate Shopping Center and Restaurant**
  Since the 1940s.

- **Tamarack Inn**
  A 1980 restaurant converted to a B&B in 1995.

- **Tollgate Trail Finders**
  A private snowmobile club.

Tollgate Store

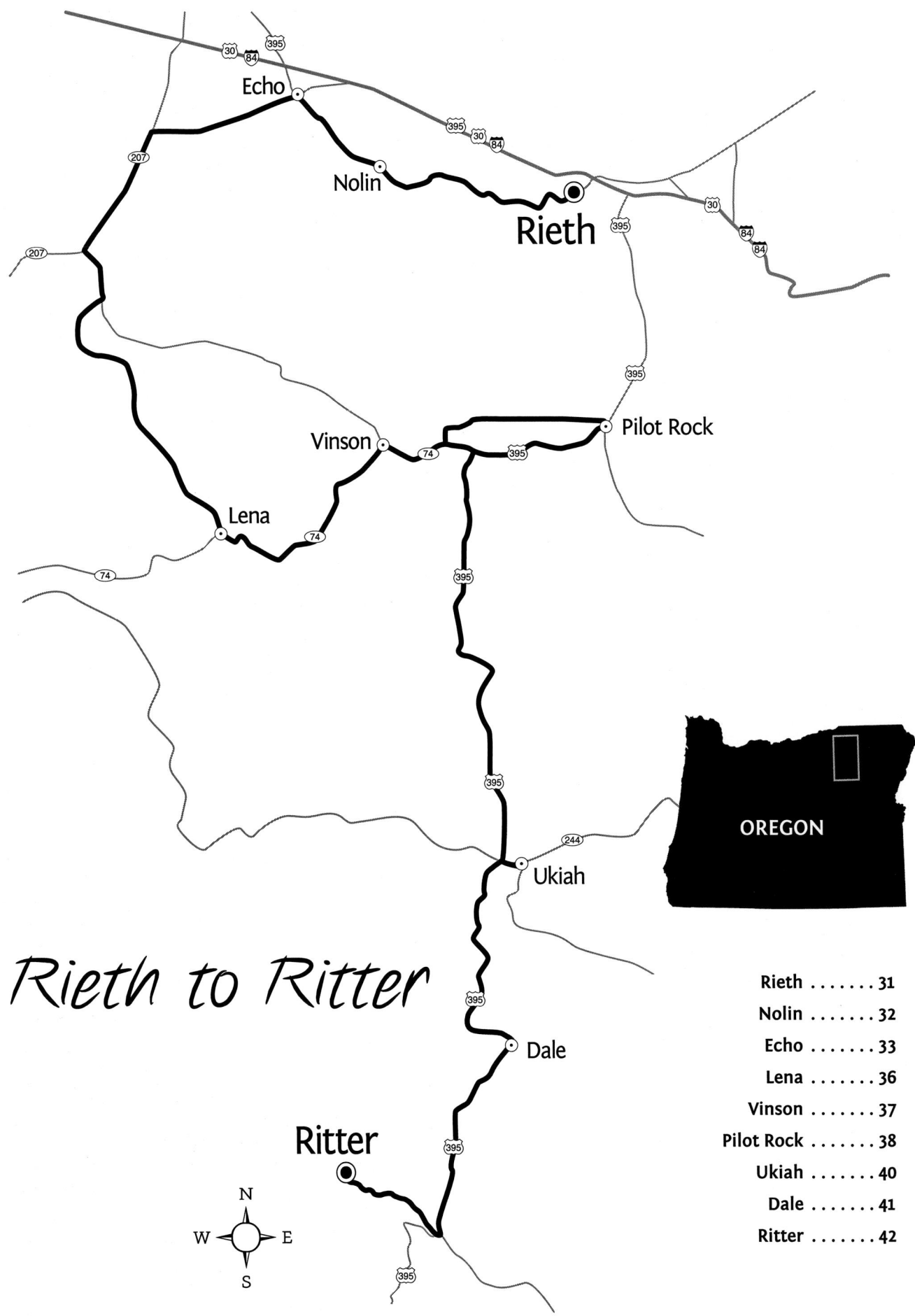

Pioneer Echoes, Pilot Rocks and Hot Springs

Rieth to Ritter (156 miles)

This route begins at the small community of Rieth, once a thriving service and repair center for the Union Pacific Railroad. From Interstate 84, take exit 207 and proceed 1.4 miles west on the Old Pendleton River Highway that follows the Umatilla River. Before entering the community of Rieth, you will pass the Blue Mountain Lumber Company. From there, basalt cliffs line the roadway from Rieth to Echo, where wagon ruts can be seen today.

Echo, located on the Oregon Trail, was home to Fort Henrietta, a military fort constructed in 1851. At La Grande, some pioneers broke from the recognized trail and traveled toward the easily recognized land form named Pilot Rock, a huge basalt rock formation resembling a ship.

The community of Pilot Rock, home to a band of gypsies in the early 1900s, suffered much damage as a result of a major fire in the 1930s. From Pilot Rock, travel through the communities of Ukiah and Dale, and end at Ritter Hot Springs, a rustic retreat, where many people relax and enjoy a therapeutic swim in natural, geothermic waters.

the road between Vinson and Pilot Rock

Rieth

Elevation: 1128 feet

Location:
45.66.111 W • 118.87.028 N

Services: food

Rieth was named after the Rieth family, pioneer settlers who made residence near the Umatilla River. The post office opened in 1916 under the name of 'Reith' and closed in 1971. Rieth was a thriving service and repair center for the Union Pacific until 1951. The small community is located on or very near the Oregon Trail. Rieth used to have a mercantile, café, grocery store, and gas station. The community has many smaller homes, which were built for the mill workers and railroad employees.

Points of Interest

- **Rieth School** *(Hill and Peter St.)*
  Constructed in 1917, the old school is now a private residence. The homeowner has converted the lower floor into a garage.

- **Old Service Station Garage** *(Main Street)*
  The garage and other buildings were constructed along this highway when it was the main road to Portland.

- **Riethhouse Bar and Grill** *(43315 Main)*
  In business for many years. There are several old buildings adjacent to the restaurant. The larger structure housed the Rieth Mercantile.

old service station garage

Rieth to Nolin

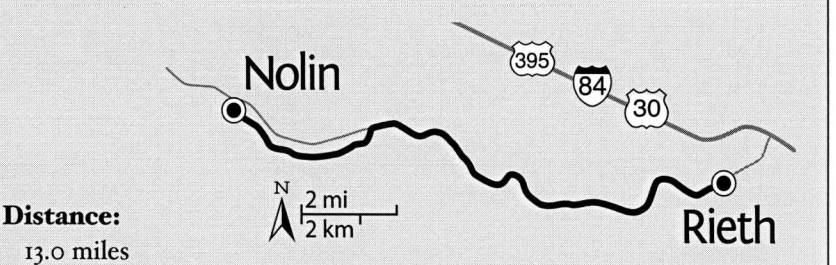

Distance: 13.0 miles

Directions:
Drive west toward Echo on the Old Pendleton River Highway.

Points En Route

(mileage from Main and Hill)

This road follows the railroad tracks and meanders through a narrow cut in the basalt cliffs carved by the Umatilla River.

0.4 miles:
Old barn.

0.9 miles:
Former gas station and site of Barnhardt. Named for an early sheep rancher, Barnhardt had a post office that opened in 1897.

3.2 miles:
Rock quarry.

5.8 miles:
The concrete skeleton of an abandoned building.

12.5 miles:
Turn left onto Mac Hoke Road and cross the Umatilla River.

12.6 miles:
Pavement turns to gravel.

12.8 miles:
Crossing railroad tracks.

13.0 miles:
Nolin

cliff wall along the road to Nolin

Nolin

Elevation: 730 feet

Location:
45.68.333 N • 119.09.944 W

Services: none

Nolin was an important stage stop in the 1860s and is located at the intersection of Mac Hoke Road and Cunningham Road. A grain elevator, several shop buildings, the school marm's house and the old hotel (now a private home) are all that remain of this small community. Signs near the cemetery and school marm's house warn of rattlesnakes. The old school was located where the shop buildings are currently located. Nolin was an important railroad-shipping center for wool and grain and once had a mercantile, livery stable and train depot.

Points of Interest

- **School Marm's House**
  (Cunningham Road)
  Located at the foot of the hill that leads to the cemetery near the Dead End sign.

- **Nolin Cemetery**
  (Cunningham Road)
  Dating to 1869, the cemetery is located on the hill above the grain elevators.

- **Nolin Stage Stop and Hotel**
  Now a private residence.

- **Nolin Grain Elevator**
  Owned and operated by the Cunningham Sheep Company.

Nolin Grain Elevator

Nolin to Echo

Distance:
7.0 miles

Directions:
Return to Old Pendleton River Highway (Rieth Road).

Points En Route

(mileage from the intersection of Cunningham Road and Mac Hoke Road near the railroad tracks)

0.4 miles:
The Umatilla River.

0.8 miles:
Nolin Cemetery visible to the left.

1.8 miles:
Irrigation dam.

3.5 miles:
Old farmhouse and outbuildings. Stretches of the old road are seen.

5.7 miles:
Irrigation ditch.

6.0 miles:
Older farmhouse.

6.7 miles:
A barn advertises "Dr. Pierce's Golden Medical Discovery," first painted in 1910.

6.8 miles:
Grave of David Koontz (no relation to the founder of Echo), one of many pioneers who lost their lives on the westward journey.

7.0 miles:
Echo

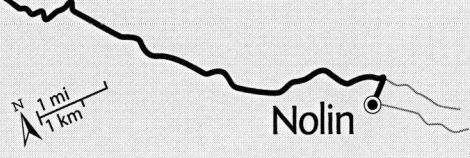

Echo

Elevation: 643 feet

Location:
45.74.196 N • 119.19.412 W

Services: gas, food, RV Park

Echo was named after the eldest daughter of Mr. and Mrs. James Koontz, early settlers in the community. A picture of the daughter hangs in the museum. Mr. Koontz, who made his fortune as a merchant in Umatilla City, moved here due to its location on the Oregon Trail and because Echo would become a stop along the railroad line. Echo is located near the site of Fort Henrietta, which was named after the wife of Major Granville Haller, who commanded troops in the early Indian campaigns. The fort was constructed in 1851, and burned to the ground during the 1855 war with the Yakima Indians. The Oregon Trail, which ran through town, crossed the Umatilla River here as early as 1847. Fording the river at this location was easy as the water moves slowly and depths are very shallow in the fall. Echo was founded in 1881 and incorporated in 1904. Mr. Koontz built a store, saloon, and flourmill. By 1890, Echo had fifteen thriving businesses. Sheep farming was a major industry in the early 1900s, due in part to knowledgeable and experienced immigrants. In 1910 Echo had a population of over 850. An irrigation project in the 1970s helped Echo find new life as an agricultural community and brought many improvements to the city. Echo, at one time, had a fifty-room hotel, which unfortunately burned in the 1920s. At the time, it was the largest hotel between Pendleton and The Dalles.

former Bank of Echo, now the Echo Museum

Points of Interest

- **City Hall** (20 S Bonanza)
  Built in 1916 and totally renovated in 1999. Prior to renovation, the downstairs housed the Star Theater and upstairs a large dance hall. Open to the public Monday through Friday.

- **Chinese House** (100 N Bonanza)
  Chinese railroad workers stayed in this house that was built in 1882.

- **VFW Hall #40**
  (Bridge and Dupont)
  The hall was moved to this site in 1901.

- **Echo Jail** (Bridge and Dupont)
  The 1865 jail and old fire equipment are displayed in the park. The building was also used as a smokehouse. Picnic area and restrooms.

- **Echo Mercantile**
  (Main and Dupont)
  Built in 1910 as a hardware store. It is now the post office.

- **Liesegang House**
  (Main and Dupont)
  Ed Liesegang came to town as a butcher and built this home in 1917.

- **C and D Garage**
  (Main and Dupont)
  Old gas pumps and a service bay.

- **ThomsonHouse**
  (Sprague and Dupont)
  Thomson was the owner of the first telephone company and served the community as mayor.

- **Echo Restaurant** (131 W Main)
  Known as the Arlington House in 1886, and later as the Echo Hotel and Saloon. Mint condition coffins were recently found on the third floor that once housed the undertaker business.

- **Koontz Building** (*141 W Main*)
  Owned and constructed by James Koontz, the 1904 building served as a mercantile, hostelry and flourmill.

- **Bank of Echo** (*230 W Main*)
  Constructed in 1920 by Joseph Cunha. Now used as a museum. A picture of Echo Koontz is displayed here.

Fort Henrietta Blockhouse

- **Site of Fort Henrietta** (*300 W Main*)
  Built in 1851 and destroyed in 1855. A replica of the blockhouse is in the city park.

- **Edwards Building** (*320 W Main*)
  One of Echo's oldest buildings, this 1883 structure originally housed the newspaper office. It is an apartment building today.

- **Umatilla Masonic Lodge #40** (*200 S Dupont*)
  Constructed and formerly located in Umatilla City, then disassembled and relocated in Echo in 1906.

- **Koontz House** (*210 N Dupont*)
  The 1881 home of town founder James Koontz.

- **Stanfield House** (*middle of 200 block on N Dupont*)
  Ralph Stanfield organized the first bank and was the Head Cashier and Business Manager. He led the city council and also acted as postmaster.

- **Thomson House** (*301 N Dupont*)
  Constructed in 1905 for Oscar Thomson, the revival home was moved to this location and completely renovated.

- **Loveridge House** (*Garden and Sprague*)
  This home was built in 1884, and was owned by a cattle baron and merchant.

- **Sullivan, Edwards and Young House** (*200 block of Garden*)
  All of these small bungalow homes were constructed about 1884 for early Echo businessmen.

- **Frendig House** (*on Theilson near the tracks*)
  Built in 1887 for the town blacksmith.

- **St. Peter's Catholic Church** (*Marble and Leezer*)
  Constrcuted in 1913. An ornate, faux marble altar and statuary adorn the nave.

- **Echo Methodist-Episcopal Church** (*1 Bonanza*)
  Built in 1886 on land donated by James Koontz. A wing and tower were added in 1910.

horse drawn equipment at Fort Henrietta

- **Dorn Building** (*between Bonanza and Dupont on Bridge*)
  Constructed in 1908 for Dr. Dorn, physician and surgeon.

- **Chinese House and Railroad Museum** (*at the corner of Bridge and Bonanza*)
  The original 1883 bunkhouse for Chinese railroad workers now houses the tools and artifacts found in a railroad excavation site.

St. Peter's Catholic Church

Echo to Lena

Distance:
35.3 miles

Directions:
Drive south on the Echo-Lexington Highway.

Points En Route

(mileage from the Umatilla River Bridge and the Oregon Trail Fort Henrietta Museum) Travel south toward Lexington.

0.1 miles:
Joseph Cunha Farmstead. The 1902 farm consists of thirteen structures.

2.6 miles:
Whitehouse Road. Go approximately 200 yards west and look for visible Oregon Trail Wagon Ruts. The ruts can be viewed on both sides of the road. Slender white stakes mark the trail, which is located on private property.

5.7 miles:
Trail Site Marker. More wagon ruts are visible at Echo Meadows Trail Site and viewpoint kiosk, 0.6 miles. A one-mile hike (round trip) on an asphalt path takes you to the ruts, also identified with slender white stakes. The early pioneers camped at this site and viewed the first frame built house since leaving Missouri.

7.9 miles:
Intersection with Highway 207. Turn left onto Highway 207.

12.0 miles:
Myers Feed and Grain Company, since 1878.

15.1 miles:
Entering Morrow County.

15.2 miles:
Go left on Butter Creek Road.

18.3 miles:
Intersection with Little Butter Creek Road. Turn right onto Little Butter Creek Road. This intersection was the site of Pine City, which was settled in 1851.

18.4 miles:
The Pine Ranch.

20.0 miles:
Intersection with Little Butter Creek and Myers Roads. Stay on Little Butter Creek Road toward Lena.

20.5 miles:
Galloway School and Community Site. The post office opened in 1886 and closed in 1915. It was named after an early settler.

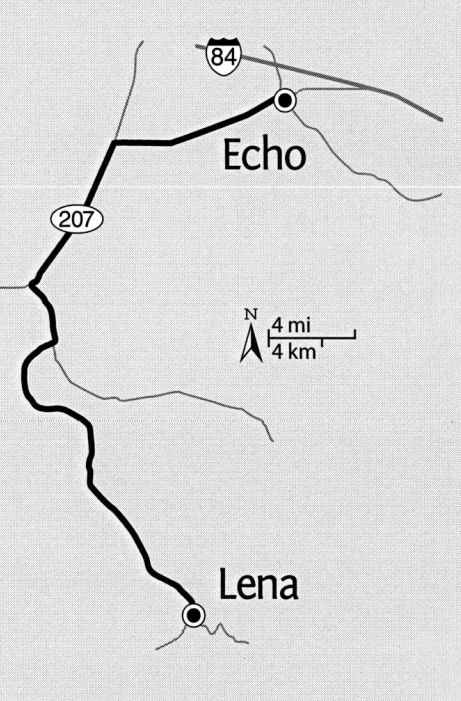

30.9 miles:
Pleasant Point Cemetery. Numerous burials date to September 1877. Gravestones indicate five Crawford children, Allie, Ella, Archie, Willie and Elric, all died in the same week. Also of note is the burial site of H. Hale, killed by Indians on July 6, 1878. There are many wooden grave markers in this small cemetery.

35.3 miles:
Lena

Oregon Train wagon ruts

Lena

Elevation: 2422 feet

Location:
45.23.944 N • 119.16.969 W

Services: none

Little remains of the small community of Lena, named by J.S. Vinson and C.E Hinton, because it was pleasant sounding. The post office opened in 1873.

"Downtown" Lena

Lena to Vinson

Distance:
14.3 miles

Directions:
Drive east on Highway 74 toward Pilot Rock.

Points En Route

(mileage from the intersection of Little Butter Creek Road and Highway 74)

0.3 miles:
Crossing Little Butter Creek. Stay left on Highway 74.

1.5 miles:
Grand view of Little Butter Creek Road as it winds through the canyon.

4.1 miles:
The summit of Franklin Hill, elevation 3456 feet.

10.7 miles:
Umatilla County.

14.3 miles.
Vinson

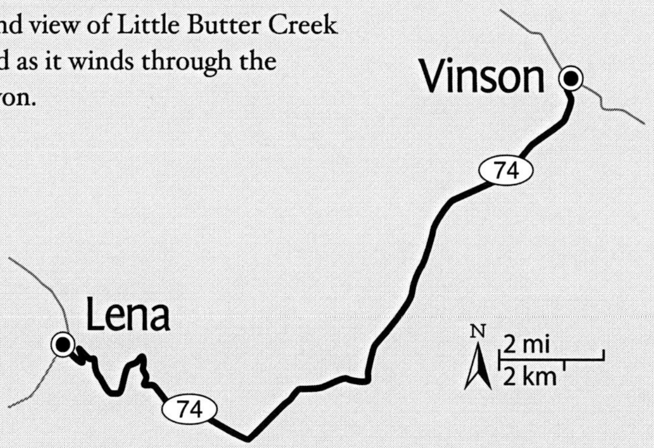

Little Butter Creek Road

Vinson

Elevation: 1978 feet

Location:
45.28.039 N • 119.05.668 W

Services: none

Texas, Oklahoma and Oregon are the only states with communities named Vinson. Vinson is named after John S. Vinson, a pioneer who settled here in 1854 where he owned and operated a general store and later served as postmaster in 1873. The post office originally opened as Butter Creek and was changed to Vinson in 1881. John Vinson located the post office in his store. Vinson was an important stage stop on the Pendleton to The Dalles route, which abruptly ended when the town was by-passed by the railroad. The old school building (now a private residence), a convenience store/gas station and several homes are all that remain of this community.

vintage gas station pump

old barn

old windmill

Vinson to Pilot Rock

Distance:
option one: 13.1 miles, paved
option two: 15.5 miles, 10 mi. gravel

Directions:
For either option, continue on Highway 74, heading east toward Pilot Rock.

Points En Route

(mileage from the intersection of Gurdane and Highway 74)

4.3 miles : *option one*
Continue 8.8 miles on Highway 74 to Pilot Rock. Information about Nye and Points En Route will appear in the Pilot Rock to Ukiah section. This route is paved.

4.3 miles: *option two*
(for the adventurous) Turn left onto Alkali Canyon Road. This route includes 10.2 miles of gravel and is closed to the public from December 1 to March 31.

Option 2 Points En Route

(mileage from the intersection of Alkali Canyon Road and Highway 74) Travel north.

5.3 miles:
Turn right onto Stock Drive Road.

11.3 miles:
Old windmill and round-roofed structure.

14.5 miles:
Pavement returns at the intersection with Mill Road. Continue straight on R.A. Koch Road.

14.8 miles:
The Bike Pit, a motocross park.

15.0 miles:
Pilot Rock Gun Club.

15.5 miles:
Pilot Rock

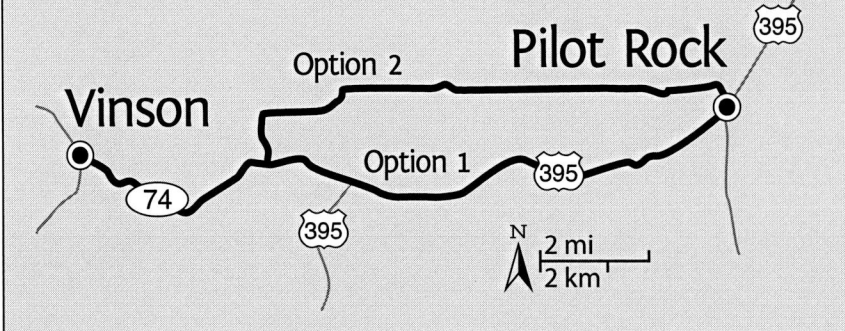

Pilot Rock

Elevation: 1662 feet

Location:
45.28.356 N • 118.50.121 W

Services: gas, food

A large basalt bluff that rises above the community gives Pilot Rock its name. It was an important point of reference for pioneers as they moved from Emigrant Pass to The Dalles. The Pilot Rock post office opened in 1868, the town was platted in 1876 and incorporated in 1911. Grain and cattle are the largest industries. In the early 1900s, a band of gypsies camped in wagons near the southern edge of town and frequented the community. A flood in 1938 did extensive damage to the downtown core area and a 1939 fire damaged or destroyed most of what was left. Pilot Rock is an agricultural community with one operational lumber mill.

Pilot Rock above town

Points of Interest

- **Presbyterian Church** *(SW Birch and 3rd)*
  Built in 1912. Now the Church of Pilot Rock.

- **City Park** *(next to Pilot Rock Elementary School on Vern McGowan Drive)*
  Restrooms, picnic and playground.

- **Old School** *(SW Birch and 4th)*
  Built in 1901 and designated Public School District #1.

- **Pilot Rock Bank** *(194 W Main)*
  Now Anne's Restaurant, the bank collapsed during the depression, closing in 1927. There is an old vault with inspection stickers on the doors.

- **Pilot Rock Mercantile** *(188 W Main)*
  Constructed in the 1920s as a grocery and mercantile store.

- **Pilot Rock Hardware** *(182 W Main)*
  This was the location of the original Pilot Rock Hardware store.

- **Stage Stop and Hotel** *(118 W Main)*
  Built in 1898 as the old stage stop and hotel, later used as a pharmacy and second-floor hospital.

- **Veterans Memorial Park** *(Main)*
  A small park with picnic facilities.

Presbyterian Church

Pilot Rock to Ukiah

Distance:
33.8 miles

Directions:
Travel south on Highway 395 to Ukiah.

Points En Route

(mileage from Birch and Main)

4.6 miles:
Remains of an old farm, windmill and outbuildings.

7.7 miles:
At the intersection of Highways 395 and 74 is the community of Nye, named for early resident A.W. Nye. A post office opened here in 1887 and closed in 1917.

17.4 miles:
Snow zone, carry chains in the winter.

17.8 miles:
Webb Slough.

18.1 miles:
Abandoned farm and outbuildings.

19.6 miles:
Conifers appear in the landscape.

21.0 miles:
Battle Mountain Scenic Corridor and historical marker. The mountain was named following the 1878 skirmish with the Bannock Indians. It was the last major uprising against the whites by the Bannocks.

22.3 miles:
Battle Mountain State Park. Day use only. Constructed as a Civilian Conservation Corps Camp. There is a giant fireplace located near the center of the park.

23.3 miles:
Battle Mountain summit – 4270 feet.

27.8 miles:
Cooper Creek.

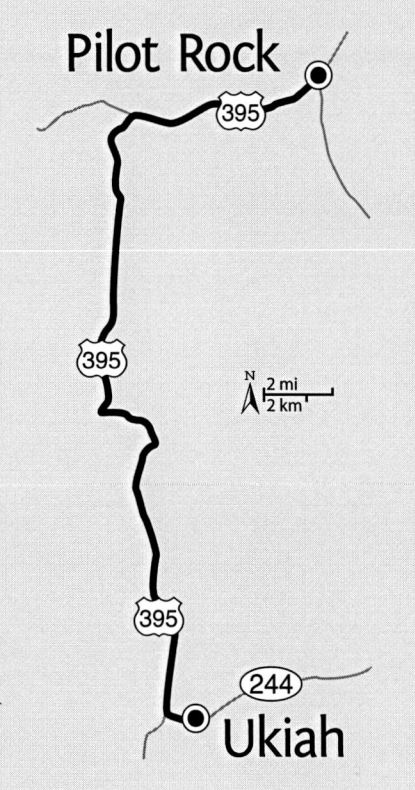

31.2 miles:
Log cabin.

32.8 miles:
Intersection of Highways 395 and 244. Turn left onto Highway 244 toward Ukiah.

33.8 miles:
Ukiah

Ukiah Antler Inn

farm house near Ukiah

Ukiah

Elevation: 3356 feet

Location:
45.08.068 N • 118.55.806 W

Services: gas, food, RV, lodging

Ukiah has always been a timber industries community. The post office opened in 1890, and the town was platted that same year, organized by the Camas Land Company. The word Ukiah comes from a similar place in California that was named for the Yokaia Indians. The US Forest Service is the largest employer in this small community, with tourism playing a major role in its economy. Ukiah Oregon is the name of the hero, written about by Wen Spencer, in his four book series of science fiction novels. The town did not officially incorporate until 1969. Ukiah caters to outdoor enthusiasts, especially people that hunt, fish and snowmobile.

Points of Interest

- **Ukiah Presbyterian Church** *(Alba and Main)*
  One of the older buildings in the community.

- **City Park** *(Alba and Main)*
  Tennis, picnic, covered area, playground equipment, information kiosk and restrooms.

- **US Forest Service**
  The Headquarters for the North Fork John Day and Umatilla National Forest Service are located at the west entrance to town.

Ukiah to Dale

Distance:
  15.5 miles

Directions:
  Return to the junction of Highways 395 and 244.

Points En Route

(mileage from Ukiah Store)

1.0 miles:
  Junction of Highways 395 and 244. Turn left, heading south, on Highway 395.

1.2 miles:
  Ukiah-Dale Scenic Corridor.

2.3 miles:
  Ukiah-Dale State Park. Camp, picnic, fish, and hike.

8.3 miles:
  Bridge Creek Wildlife area.

12.1 miles:
  Camas Creek.

13.5 miles:
  The 45th parallel, halfway between the North Pole and the Equator.

14.8 miles:
  Crossing the John Day River, Oregon's longest river without a dam.

15.0 miles:
  Entering Grant County.

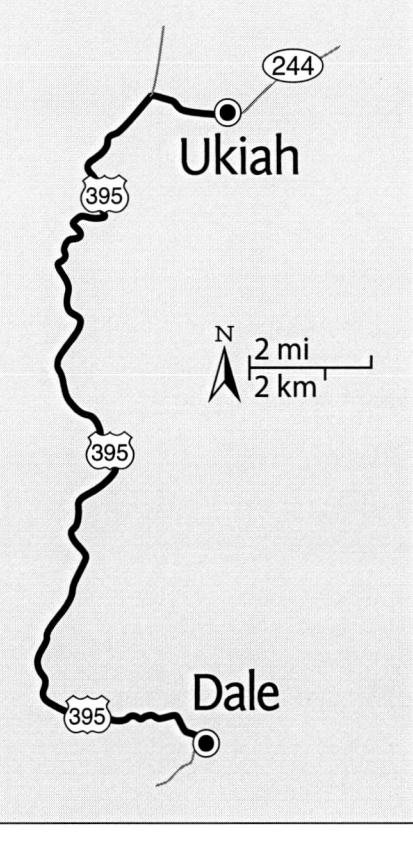

15.5 miles:
  Dale

no dumping near Ukiah

Dale

Elevation: 3240 feet

Location:
44.59.304 N • 118.56.879 W

Services: gas, groceries

Dale was originally called Dorman, after 1887 postmaster James W. Dorman. The name was changed to Dale in 1891, one year before the store opened. This small community of several homes, a store and a game cooler, is located near the John Day River. Little remains of this community that is economically dependent upon tourism, recreation and the forest industry.

Point of Interest

- **Dale Store**
  Opened and continuously operated since 1892.

Dale Service Station

Dale to Ritter Hot Springs

Distance:
21.4 miles

Directions:
Continue South on Highway 395.

Points En Route

(mileage from the Dale Store)

5.6 miles:
Meadowbrook Lodge.

6.4 miles:
Meadowbrook Summit, elevation 4127 feet.

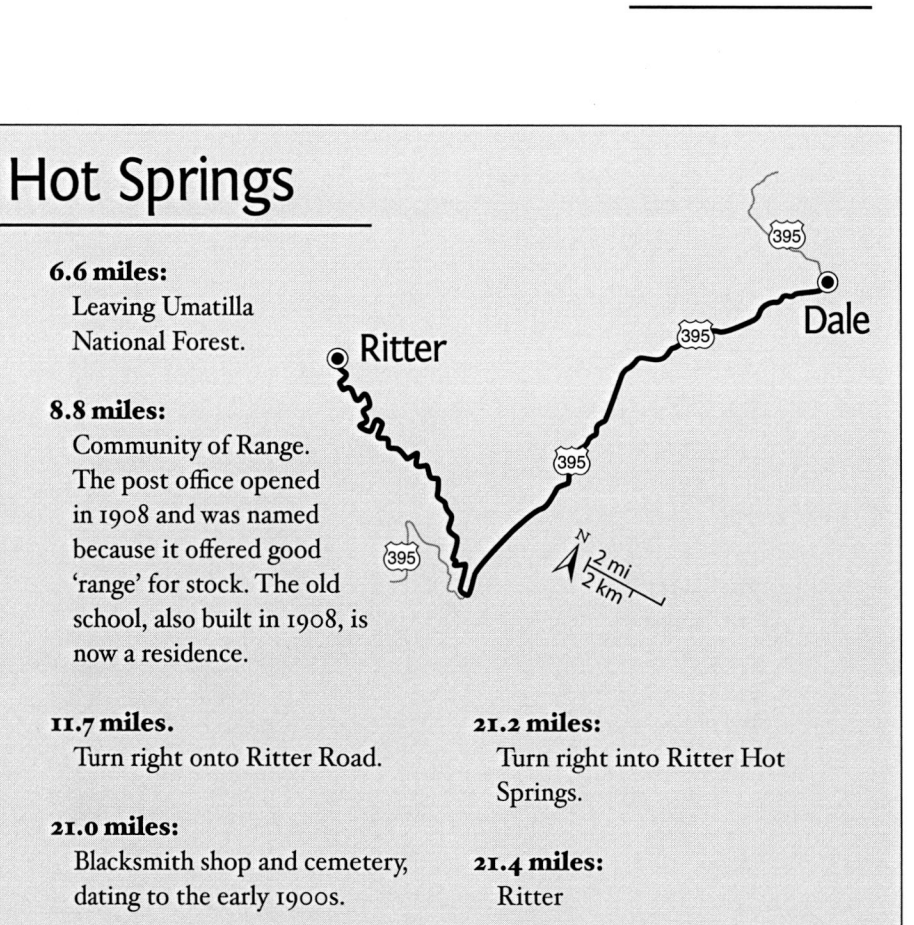

6.6 miles:
Leaving Umatilla National Forest.

8.8 miles:
Community of Range. The post office opened in 1908 and was named because it offered good 'range' for stock. The old school, also built in 1908, is now a residence.

11.7 miles.
Turn right onto Ritter Road.

21.0 miles:
Blacksmith shop and cemetery, dating to the early 1900s.

21.2 miles:
Turn right into Ritter Hot Springs.

21.4 miles:
Ritter

Ritter Hot Springs

Elevation: 3490 feet

Location:
44.89.211 N • 119.14.347 W

Services: food, camping, lodging

William McDuffee, a freight hauler between the John Day and Umatilla gold mines, discovered the hot springs in the 1870s and named them McDuffee Hot Springs. The name of the community was later changed to Ritter for the Reverend Joseph Ritter, a Baptist minister, who allowed the first post office to be established in his home in 1886. Ritter was a stage stop along the Pendleton to John Day route. Time seems to have stood still at the quaint Ritter Hot Springs retreat that is open from Memorial Day through Labor Day. The water in the swimming pool is kept at a constant 85 degrees and the four therapeutic pools, located across the river, are maintained at about 105 degrees. The pool was constructed where the old dance hall stood. The therapeutic pools were constructed in the early 1900s. Fires, the latest occurring in 1951, destroyed two hotels. The Ritter School, built in 1907, is now lost to time and the elements. Stellerite, a highly sought rock crystal, can be found in the area.

Ritter General Store

Points of Interest

- **Ritter General Store**
  Dates to 1894.

- **Ritter Hot Springs Resort**
  Opened in the 1880s and once was a year around operation.

- **Log Cabin**
  Next to the creek, was constructed circa 1902.

- **Ritter Hotel**
  The rustic hotel, with inexpensive rates, was built in the 1910s.

Log cabin

Ritter Hotel

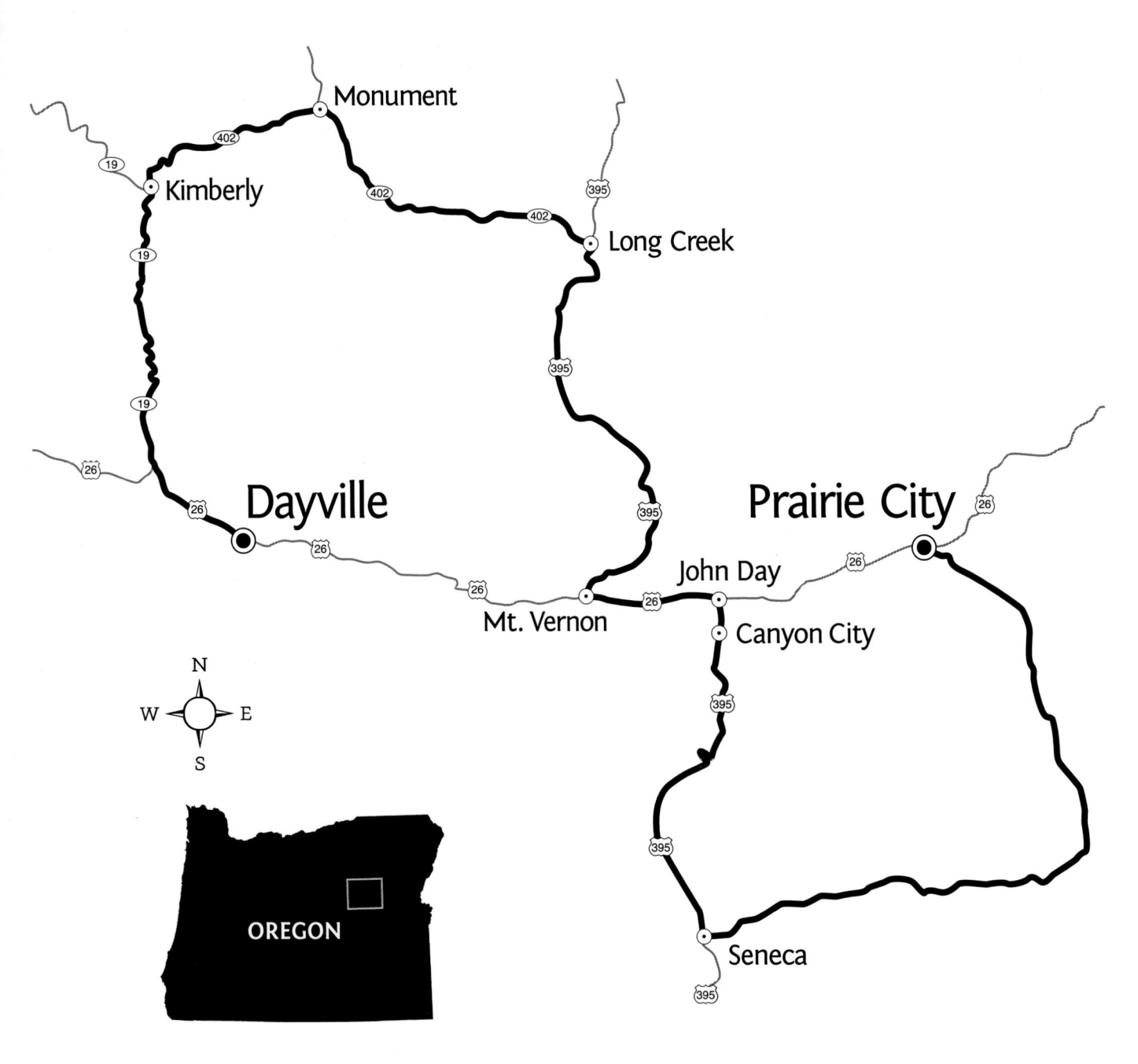

Prairie City to Dayville

Prairie City	45
Seneca	47
Canyon City	48
John Day	49
Mt. Vernon	51
Long Creek	53
Monument	55
Kimberly	56
Dayville	58

Gold, Chinese Medicine and Metasequoia

Prairie City to Dayville (221 miles)

Several of Oregon's most scenic areas, including the Strawberry Mountain Wilderness Area and the John Day Fossil Beds, are explored along this route. Beginning in Prairie City, where gold was discovered in 1862, the trip progresses through the Strawberry Mountains and the Malheur National Forest to Seneca, known for its cold temperatures and yellow pine forests.

Continue toward Canyon City, the largest town in 1863 Oregon, due to the 1862 discovery of gold. Move on to Canyon City's sister city, John Day, home to the Chinese Kam Wah Chung Company. From John Day, travel to Mount Vernon, a city settled on the old Fort Dalles Military Road and named after a racehorse.

Journey to Long Creek, known for its former lawlessness and rowdiness, en route to Monument, named for the huge rock formation that towers above the town. The trip ends in Dayville, gateway to the John Day Fossil Beds National Monument and the home of the Dayville Mercantile, in operation since 1896.

Picture Gorge between Kimberly and Dayville

Prairie City

Elevation: 3595 feet

Location:
44.27.717 N • 118.42.786 W

Services: gas, food, lodging, RV, B&B

Legend tells of women washing clothes in Dixie Creek, an area located three miles from current Prairie City, only to discover gold in its sandy bottom. Miners that hailed from the south named the settlement Dixie. The gold quickly played out and the miners moved down river where Dixie Creek emptied into the John Day River. It was on this 'prairie' that the community of Prairie City was formed. The first sawmill, built in 1862, milled the lumber used in the 1865 construction of Fort Logan, where a garrison of over 200 men was stationed. The first saloon opened in 1868, the Prairie City post office in 1870, and the town incorporated in 1891. Prairie City endured major fires in 1884, 1887 and 1901. The first school opened in 1876 and burned in the 1901 fire. The Sumpter Valley Railroad, charted in 1890, was primarily used to haul timber to mining areas. Formal passenger service ended in 1937, forcing occasional travelers to ride in the freight train caboose until 1947 when the rail line was discontinued.

view down Main Street

Points of Interest

- **IOOF Hall** *(Front and McHaley)*
  Constructed after the fire in 1902.

- **Masonic Lodge** *(Front and Main)*
  Built in 1911.

- **Shonshoni Winds Tavern**
  (118 Front)
  Circa 1891.

- **Prairie City Pharmacy**
  (124 Front)
  Old newspapers are used as wallpaper in this 1890 Stage Stop.

- **American Legion log cabin**
  (307 Front)
  Near the Forest Service building.

- **Old homes**
  (115 Main, 140 Main, 226 Main, 205 Johnson, 582 Bridge, and 778 Bridge)
  All built around the turn of the century.

- **DeWitt Depot Museum**
  (Main and Bridge)
  Located in the 1910 two-story train depot.

- **Strawberry Grange #661**
  (corner of 4th and McHaley)
  Built in the 1910s.

- **Prairie City Methodist Church** *(211 6th)*
  The oldest church in the community, built in 1907.

- **Prairie City Park**
  (6th between McHaley and Bridge)
  Playground, restrooms, and picnic area.

- **Prairie City School**
  (10th and Overholt)
  Built in 1910 and still in use.

- **Strawberry Mountain Bed and Breakfast (1910)**
  Located east of town, the B&B was built in 1910 by Rice McHaley, Grant County Judge. The judge's 1890 home, where he raised horses for the US Cavalry, is located west of the B&B.

- **Site of Camp Logan**
  A military fort, located five miles south of town, was constructed in 1865, and operated until 1869.

DeWitt Depot Museum

Prairie City to Seneca

Distance:

46.2 miles

Directions:
From the intersection of Main and Bridge (where Prairie City Road begins), go left on Bridge, heading east on Prairie City Road.

Points En Route

(mileage from Main and Bridge, near the DeWitt Museum)

The next forty miles, which pass through the Strawberry Mountains and the Malhuer National Forest, afford hiking, snow mobiling, fishing, hunting, picnicking, and camping. Bear, cougar, eagle and big horned sheep are frequently spotted and 378 species of birds have been identified in the forest.

0.1 miles:
Prairie City Cemetery. Dates to 1870s.

1.2 miles:
Old farmhouse.

7.1 miles:
Intersection with Forest Road 2635. Continue on Prairie City Road.

9.9 miles:
Abandoned ranch.

10.6 miles:
Excellent view of the forested Strawberry Mountains.

11.7 miles:
Entering Malhuer National Forest.

13.3 miles:
Sunshine Trail Head.

14.5 miles:
Trout Farm Forest Campground. Primitive facilities.

16.2 miles:
Crescent Campground. Primitive.

16.5 miles:
Leaving Malhuer National Forest.

18.8 miles:
Skyline Trail.

19.5 miles:
Huddleston Snow Park and restrooms.

21.8 miles:
The Meadows.

21.9 miles:
Intersection with National Forest Road 16. Turn right onto Forest Road 16, heading toward Seneca.

24.6 miles:
Intersection with Summit Creek Road. Stay on Forest Road 16.

27.1 miles:
Summit, 5106 feet.

27.8 miles:
Big Creek Campground.

28.9 miles:
Wildlife viewing turnout.

30.4 miles:
Stay on Forest Road 16.

35.4 miles:
Intersection with Forest Road 15. Stay on Forest Road 16.

35.6 miles:
Parrish Cabin Campground.

41.3 miles:
Ranch with several log outbuildings.

46.2 miles:
Seneca

old wagon near Prairie City

Seneca

Elevation: 4666 feet

Location:
44.08.242 N • 118.58.359 W

Services: food, lodging, RV

In 1895, the year the post office opened, Postmaster Minnie Southworth named the community to honor her uncle, Judge Seneca Smith of Portland. For years Seneca was home to the Hines Lumber Company, a major producer of yellow pine wood products. Located in Bear Valley, Seneca had a recorded temperature of −54 degrees F. A 1981 fire destroyed the old store, restaurant, dance hall, barbershop and other old buildings.

Seneca School

Points of Interest:

- **Bearcat Lodge** *(109 Barnes)*
  On Highway 395 near the park. Two bobcats, Big and Bob, are caged next to the 1935 CCC Forest Service lodge.

- **Seneca School** *(3rd and Park)*
  The K-8 school opened in 1929.

- **Seneca City Park**
  (4th and Barnes)
  Picnic, playground, ball fields, and restrooms.

- **Badminton Bird Burner**
  The Hines Lumber Company burner can be seen from the park.

- **Bear Valley Golf Course**
  The course sports a helicopter landing pad midway through the first and second holes. Golfers must drive across the Silvies River to play the third hole.

- **Row of Tidy Houses** *(Park)*
  Tree-lined street, adjacent to the park.

Seneca to Canyon City

Distance:
  22.0 miles

Directions:
  Go east on Highway 395, following signs to Canyon City.

Points En Route

(mileage from the Bearcat Lodge)

0.3 miles:
  Timbers Inn RV park and remains of the Hines Lumber Company.

4.2 miles:
  Abandoned cabin with views of the Strawberry Mountains.

9.3 miles:
  Starr Campground. Summit, 5152 feet.

14.2 miles:
  Leaving Malhuer National Forest.

20.6 miles:
  Remains of an old mining operation.

22.0 miles:
  Canyon City

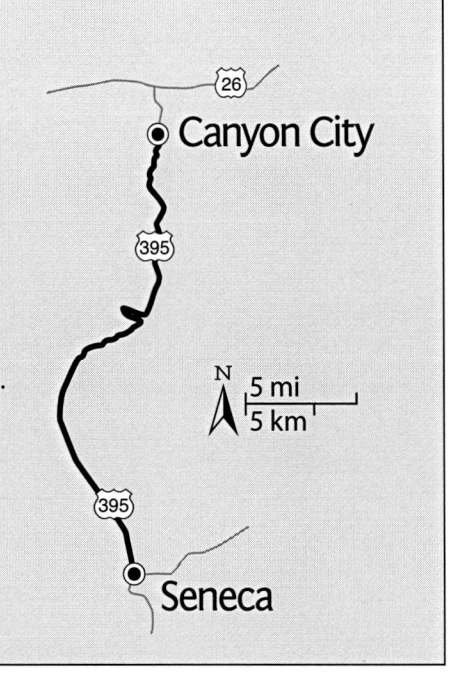

Canyon City

Elevation: 3182 feet

Location:
44.23.353 N • 118.56.993 W

Services: gas, food, lodging

GOLD! Over 800,000 ounces of gold came from Canyon Creek, the equivalent of over $700 million dollars at 2009 rates. Gold was discovered here in 1862 and the town quickly grew to over 10,000 people, making it the most populated city in 1860s Oregon. Canyon City was platted in 1862, the post office opened in 1864 when Grant County was formed, was the county seat until the courthouse burned in 1870, and incorporated in 1891. Canyon City was home to Joaquin Miller; pony express rider, lawyer, judge, journalist, miner, cattle baron, orchardist, author and poet. His cabin is part of the Grant County Historical Museum. The 1910 Greenhorn jail, part of the museum, was moved to this location in 1963. Three major fires threatened this small community, the first in 1870, the next in 1898 and the worst in 1937. The town also survived a terrible flood, which occurred in 1896. Canyon City had a large population of Chinese Americans until 1885, when city fathers intentionally burned their residences, resulting in four to six thousand Chinese workers moving to nearby John Day.

St. Thomas Episcopal Church

Points of Interest

- **Grant County Historical Museum**
  (101 Canyon City Boulevard)
  The 1865 Miller Cabin, 1910 Greenhorn Jail and mining memorabilia are displayed. Open in summer.

- **St. Thomas Episcopal Church**
  (139 Washington)
  In continual use since 1876, having survived all the fires.

- **Community Hall and Masonic Lodge #34** *(131 Washington)*
  The original lodge was destroyed in the 1937 fire. Two doors open into the 1938 replacement.

- **City Hall** *(123 Washington)*
  Rebuilt in 1938.

- **CG Guernsey Building**
  (120 Washington)
  This 1899 building survived the fires.

- **Old Houses**
  (106, 110 and 114 Washington)
  Over 100 years old and noteworthy construction.

- **Sels Brewery** *(113 Washington)*
  Opened in 1872, survived the fires.

- **Canyon City Bank**
  (Main and Washington)
  An old bank, one of several in town.

- **St. Andrews Cemetery**
  (off Main on Patterson)
  Dates to around 1876.

- **City Park** *(Main an Park)*
  Erected on the site of the Elkhorn Hotel, Grant County's finest, that was destroyed during the 1937 fire.

- **Canyon City School**
  (108 Rebel Hill)
  The name Rebel comes from southern sympathizers that settled on the hill. The 1901 school is now a private residence.

- **Boot Hill Cemetery**
  (0.8 miles up Main)
  Boot Hill (difficult to find) is located near the entrance to the Canyon City Cemetery. Five men, all hung for murder, lie in four graves. The dates of the hangings were 1863, 1865, 1888, 1889 and 1893.

Sels Brewery

John Day

Elevation: 3083 feet

Location:
44.25.010 N • 118.52.314 W

Services: gas, food, lodging, RV

Canyon City to John Day

Distance:
0.8 miles

Directions:
Travel north on Highway 395. Canyon Creek parallels the road to John Day.

In 1862, B.C. Trowbridge was the first settler in John Day, which was originally known as 'Lower Town.' In 1864, John Day prospered with a blacksmith shop, a flourmill, and two saloons. The post office opened in 1865, discontinued in 1871 and re-established in 1879. John Day incorporated in 1901 with 1800 residents. The community is named after John Day, a member of the Wilson Price Hunter Astor Overland Expedition. After joining the group in 1811, Day took more than one year to get from the Snake River to Astoria, having endured illness, robbery and beating along the way. On a return trip to St. Louis in 1812, Day went insane and later died in Idaho in 1820. The fossil beds, city, and river all bear his name. John Day is the Grant County seat. The Dalles Military Road, which extended into John Day and Canyonville, was constructed in 1868, the same time a pony express station opened in John Day. It was during the construction of this road that the Fossil Beds were discovered. Highway 19 follows much of the military road as it was originally developed. When the gold played out in the 1870s, Chinese miners were the only ones working the creeks, choosing permanent residence in the John Day area. The area economy comes from the Malhuer National Forest, agriculture, and tourism.

Kam Wah Chung and Co. Museum

Points of Interest

- **John Day Bank** *(160 E Main)*
  Opened in 1904.

- **Grant County Ranch and Rodeo Museum** *(241 E Main)*
  Much local and cowboy history.

- **The Advent Christian Church** *(261 W Main)*
  Constructed in 1878, the historic church is of Victorian Gothic Revival style. The parsonage, located behind the church building, houses the Grant County Chamber of Commerce.

John Day Bank

- **Johnson Building**
  (Main and Canyon)
  Constructed in 1902.

- **John Day Mercantile Building**
  (SE Dayton)
  Three-story construction.

- **Kam Wah Chung and Co. Museum** *(NW Canton)*
  The 1870s trading post on The Dalles Military Road became the 1888 home of Lung On and Ing Hay as well as the social and religious center for the Chinese community. The lower floor was constructed in the 1870s and the upper floor in the 1890s. It became a state park in the mid 1970s. Hay practiced herbal medicine and diagnosed patients by feeling their pulse. On was a successful merchant who sold supplies to miners before opening a dry goods store and import business. The museum is open May through October.

- **Sonshine Bed and Breakfast**
  (210 NW Canton)
  Built in 1948 as the home and office of Dr. Ing Hay.

- **John Day Elementary School**
  (Bridge and 1st)
  Opened in 1916.

- **Old House** *(175 N Canyon)*
  One of John Days older residences.

- **Grant County Fairgrounds**
  (NE 3rd)
  Since 1909. Floods seriously damaged the grounds in 1964.

- **Rest Lawn Cemetery**
  (Valley View Road)
  Go North on Bridge to Valley View. Dates to the 1870s.

- **Trowbridge Ranch**
  (north of town)
  The 1862 ranch is the oldest in the county.

- **John Day Fossil Beds**
  The deep red colors in the rock formations indicate tropical climates (high rainfall) that are 40-55 million years old and the light blue-green and tan colors (cool and dry climate) are 20-40 million years old. The state fossil plant, the Metasequoia, grew in abundance from 16-35 million years ago. Some of the oldest rocks in Oregon, 225-300 million years old, can be found in the John Day Basin.

John Day to Mt. Vernon

Distance:
6.6 miles

Directions:
Travel west on Highway 26 (the road follows the old The Dalles Military Road).

Points En Route

(mileage from the intersection of Highway 26 and Patterson Bridge Road)

0.5 miles:
Drive-in theater.

0.9 miles:
Beautiful, old, two-story home.

1.0 miles:
Malheur Lumber Company, one of the county's largest employers.

1.1 miles:
John Day Golf Club.

2.0 miles:
One of many old farmhouses built along the military road.

4.9 miles:
A stone barn, built in 1879 of rock quarried nearby, housed the famous horse, Mt. Vernon. The date is etched in stone above the front window.

5.5 miles:
Clyde Holliday State Park. The 16-acre park has restrooms, picnic and play areas, and a campground with full RV hook-ups. Holliday was a local rancher who donated the land for the park in 1960. Beaver and otter are frequently seen in the river.

6.1 miles:
McKrola Homestead. The 1870s house was built to face The Dalles Military Road. The icehouse, located next to the farmhouse, was built of rock quarried from the hill behind the farm, with two-feet of sawdust insulation in the ceiling and walls to control the temperature.

6.6 miles.
Mt Vernon

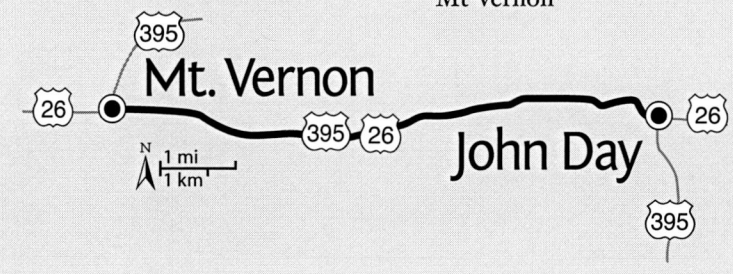

Mt Vernon

Elevation: 2838 feet

Location:
44.25.098 N • 119.06.805 W

Services: gas, food, lodging, RV

Located at the crossroads of Highway 26 and Highway 395, Mt. Vernon is named for a racehorse. A stone barn, complete with gunnery holes, was built just east of the current town to house and protect the famous horse. Mt. Vernon (the mountain) rises east of town and is visible in the distance behind the barn. The post office opened in 1877 but the town did not incorporate until 1948. The first general store was built in 1881, a phone company in 1914, and an auto repair shop in 1915. Many sawmills once dotted the area that sustained a population that exceeded today's count of 595 citizens. Agriculture, livestock and lumbering are the main industries.

McKrola Homestead barn and equipment

stone barn east of town

Points of Interest

- **Mt. Vernon Community Church** *(Main)*
  Built in 1905 on the banks of Beech Creek.

- **Fletcher Cemetery** *(go south on Ingle to East Riverside St)*
  Dates to the 1880s.

- **David Hamilton Winery** *(Ingle and Main)*
  Tasting room and sales. All Hamilton Fruit Wines are made without sulfites.

- **Mt. Vernon Hot Springs** *(2.5 miles north on Highway 395)*
  The original building was constructed in 1905, damaged by flooding in 1951 and burned to the ground in 1968. The hot springs were discovered in 1868 and reportedly had a water temperature that ranged from 108-112 degrees.

Mt. Vernon to Long Creek

Distance:
27.8 miles

Directions:
Travel north on Highway 395.

Points En Route

(mileage from the intersection of Main and N Mountain/Highway 395)

2.7 miles:
A dilapidated barn and old rail fence.

6.1 miles:
Unique stone fences.

9.5 miles:
Entering Malhuer National Forest.

10.7 miles:
Old barn, near collapse.

15.4 miles:
Leaving Malhuer National Forest.

15.7 miles:
4687 foot summit.

16.7 miles:
Two very old log structures and a barn.

18.1 miles:
Abandoned houses.

19.1 miles:
Site of 'Beech Creek.' A post office, named for the pioneer family that first settled here, opened in 1900. In 1930, there was a population of 42.

20.1 miles:
Beech Creek/Fox Cemetery.

20.9 miles:
The community of Fox, named for the animals that were found in large quantity. The Fox post office, located on Main Street, opened in 1883 and closed in 2004. Still standing is a church, complete with outhouse, the old school, the Fox store, Fox garage and gas pump, and a house built in 1879.

22.6 miles:
Entering Malhuer National Forest.

23.6 miles:
5039 foot summit. Breathtaking views of the valley.

25.3 miles:
Rest area.

25.5 miles:
Distant view of Long Creek.

27.8 miles:
Long Creek

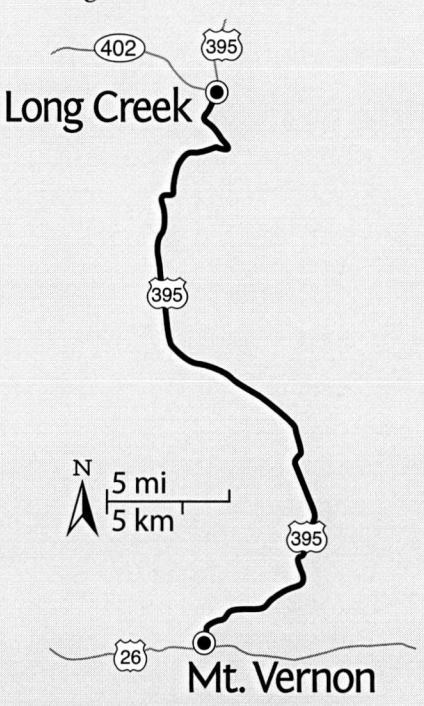

Fox Church

outhouse in Fox

52

Long Creek

Elevation: 3839 feet

Location:
44.42.775 N • 119.06.227 W

Services: groceries, lodging

Because of the Indian Wars, a fort was constructed near the site of Long Creek in 1878. The community is erroneously named in belief that Long Creek was the longest creek in Oregon. Long Creek is one of Oregon's true cow towns, where cowpokes were routinely involved in drunken brawls and shootings in the 1880s and 1890s. The post office was established in 1880, the city incorporated in 1891 and the school opened in 1916. The 1902 population of Long Creek exceeded 500 residents, compared to today's 240. At that time, Long Creek had a grocery store, drug store, jewelry store, hotel, livery stable, meat market, harness and saddle store, two general stores, two doctor's offices, and two blacksmith shops.

old house (390 Main)

Points of Interest

- **City Hall** *(2nd and Hardesty)*
  Dates to 1891, when the city incorporated.

- **Long Creek Community Church** *(2nd)*
  The oldest in Long Creek, circa 1890.

- **Old House** *(Esther and Main)*
  Long Creek's finest.

- **SDA Church** *(Bradley and Main)*
  Built as the Baptist Church.

- **Old House** *(390 Main)*
  This house, located across from the school, dates to 1890.

- **Long Creek School**
  (400 block of Main)
  Dates to 1916.

- **Long Creek City Park**
  (Main and Allen)
  Playground and picnic area.

- **Long Creek Cemetery**
  (1.25 miles east on Keeney Forks Road to Long Creek/Pass Creek Road)
  Dates to 1877.

the finest house in Long Creek

overgrown outbuilding

Long Creek to Monument

Distance:
20.5 miles

Directions:
Travel west on Highway 402.

Points En Route

(mileage from the intersection of Highway 395 and Highway 402)

1.5 miles:
Crossing Paul Creek.

1.6 miles:
Old farm and barn.

8.3 miles:
Geologic Marker. Basalt flow information.

9.7 miles:
Views of the valley.

10.9 miles:
Hamilton is a small community named for J.H. Hamilton, first settler in the area. Hamilton was a pioneer cattleman and racehorse fancier, who homesteaded here in 1874. Anson Frank built and ran the first general store. Hamilton is on the edge of the John Day Painted Hills.

11.0 miles:
Old Hamilton Store and post office.

11.1 miles:
Series of interesting outbuildings.

11.5 miles:
Hamilton Cemetery, 1892. One marker reads:

> *Rest little one, a mothers tears may fall*
>
> *But not for worlds would she her child recall.*

11.6 miles:
Red rock hillside.

12.0 miles:
Abandoned ranch.

12.6 miles:
Geologic Marker describing the "Sunken Mountain."

20.3 miles:
Crossing the John Day River.

20.5 miles:
Monument

abandoned Hamilton general store

Monument

Elevation: 2020 feet

Location:
44.49.164 N • 119.25.295 W

Services: gas, food, lodging, RV

Monument is named for a unique rock formation that resembles a pulpit. The first settlers arrived in 1852, the post office opened in 1874, the town incorporated in 1905, then dissolved and re-incorporated in 1947. Approximately 150 residents live in the community that was platted around a bend in the John Day River. Monument has a municipal airport, located one mile northwest of town.

Monument Mountain

Points of Interest

- **Monument Mountain**
  The formation can be viewed from the school grounds.

- **Boyer's Grocery and Gas** *(778 Old Highway Road)*
  Family owned since 1927. The old "Boyer's Cash Store" sign is on the west side of the building. Old photos hang on the walls inside the store.

- **Old Car Dealership** *(160 Main)*
  The former dealership and service station houses a tavern.

- **Monument Grocery** *(244 Main)*
  This grocery store was built in the 1940s.

- **Monument School** *(127 North)*
  Built in 1928 and the third school on this site.

- **Monument Park**
  (between 1st and 2nd and John Day)
  Picnic area and playground.

- **Monument Presbyterian Church** *(2nd and John Day)*
  The first services in this church were held in 1903.

- **Triangle Park** *(2nd and Wilson)*
  A small, triangular piece of property with a picnic table.

- **Old House** *(Wilson and Willow)*
  One of several Monument homes built in the late 1890s.

- **Old House** *(3rd and John Day)*
  Lumber from the local sawmill was used to build this late 19th century house.

- **Monument Lumber Mill**
  (Gorge and Park)
  The saws are quiet and only the badminton burner remains.

Monument School

55

old store front in Kimberly

Kimberly

Elevation: 1810 feet

Location:
44.45.537 N • 119.38.634 W

Services: store, post office

Kimberly was named after a well-known family who established the first orchards in the area. Kimberly is an important rafting and fishing location on the John Day River. Kimberly had a school that operated from 1929 to 1946.

Monument to Kimberly

Distance:
13.2 miles

Directions:
From the intersection of Highway 402 and John Day Street, drive west on Highway 402. The road will parallel the John Day River.

Points En Route

(mileage from the intersection of Highway 402 and John Day Street)

0.3 miles:
Monument Cemetery. Dates to the 1890s.

0.7 miles:
Top Road. (optional side trip - travel approximately five miles to the Top stage stop and school) Top had a post office in 1915 and was named after resident Top Reasner.

10.3 miles:
Big Bend Recreation Site. River access.

11.5 miles:
Lone Pine Recreation Area. Picnic and river access.

12.6 miles:
Kimberly Orchards. Over 50 years of fruit growing.

13.2 miles:
Kimberly

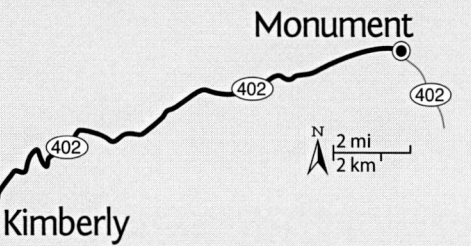

heading south out of Kimberly

Kimberly to Dayville

Distance:
24.5 miles

Directions:
Travel south on highway 19 toward Dayville.

Points En Route

(mileage from the intersection of Highway 402 and Highway 19)

0.2 miles:
Crossing the John Day River.

6.2 miles:
Old farm and buildings.

7.8 miles:
Beautiful rock formations, part of the John Day Fossil Beds National Monument Area.

8.4 miles:
John Day Fossil Beds picnic area and trailheads.

10.1 miles:
Cathedral Rock.

12.1 miles:
Land's Inn B&B access road.

12.7 miles:
John Day Fossil Beds Blue Basin.

13.9 miles:
Old ranch.

14.3 miles:
Goose Rock.

15.9 miles:
The 1890 Cant Ranch. The main house, now a museum, was built in 1917. The log cabin was constructed in 1900. Under the jurisdiction of the John Day Fossil Beds, the old ranch has exhibits, hiking trails and a picnic area. A major rock strata tilt can be seen in the hill across the river.

16.0 miles:
Thomas Condon Visitors Center.

17.7 miles:
Basalt cliffs.

17.9 miles:
Intersection of Highways 19 and 26. Turn left on Highway 26 toward Dayville.

18.0 miles:
Picture Gorge.

19.2 miles:
End Picture Gorge.

19.4 miles:
Entering wildlife migration area.

19.6 miles:
Geologic Marker – Picture Gorge.

20.3 miles:
John Day Fossil Beds Scenic Overlook.

22.3 miles:
Dayville Cemetery, dating to 1880s.

22.5 miles:
Old Dayville School, now a private residence.

24.0 miles:
C Bar C Guest Ranch.

24.5 miles:
Dayville

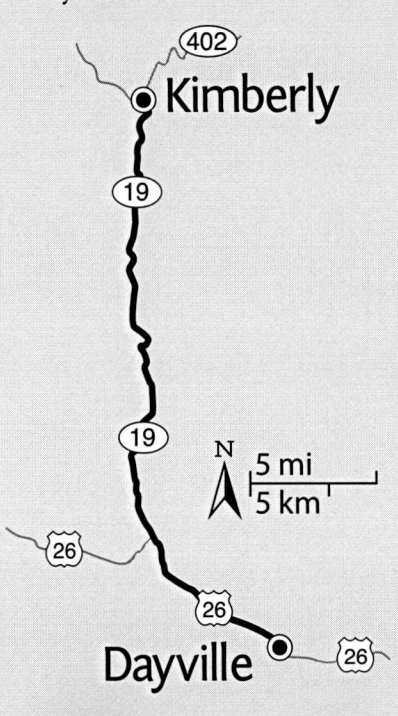

Cant Ranch with Sheep Rock behind

Picture Gorge

Dayville

Elevation: 2437 feet

Location:
44.28.210 N • 119.32.203 W

Services: gas, food, lodging, RV

This small community, named after John Day, opened its post office in 1868. The Dayville community incorporated in 1914. The old military road, which is now Highway 26 and the main road through town, is lined with many old homes. About 185 people reside in Dayville.

Dayville Mercantile

Points of Interest

- **Country Inn**
  (School House and Highway 26)
  The "A" frames were moved here from Antelope where they formerly housed the followers of Rahjneesh Purham.

- **Cap Lewis House**
  (280 School House)
  The oldest house in Dayville, located diagonally across from the school.

- **Dayville Park**
  (Franklin and Highway 26)
  Restrooms, tennis, playground, horseshoes, and picnic.

- **City Hall**
  (Franklin across from the park)
  Cell bars can still be found in the 1898 building, formerly a jail and later used as a telephone office.

- **Dayville Mercantile**
  (207 Franklin)
  Continuously operating as a grocery/mercantile since 1896. In 1898, a saloon occupied part of the store.

- **Dayville Community Hall**
  (240 Franklin)
  Built in 1920 as a movie theater and dance hall. The old carbon arc projector can be found inside the hall.

- **Old Church** *(Franklin)*
  Now a private residence. The school district acquired the church and property, sold it, and through an endowment, provides college scholarships for all of its high school graduates.

- **Old Dayville Gas Station**
  (Highway 26)
  The station phone number was 9672.

- **Post Office** *(across from the RV park on Highway 26)*
  This was the site of the Pony Express Depot.

- **Dayville Presbyterian Church**
  (S. Fork and Millie Way)
  Church services were first held in 1915.

Dayville Schools

Post Office

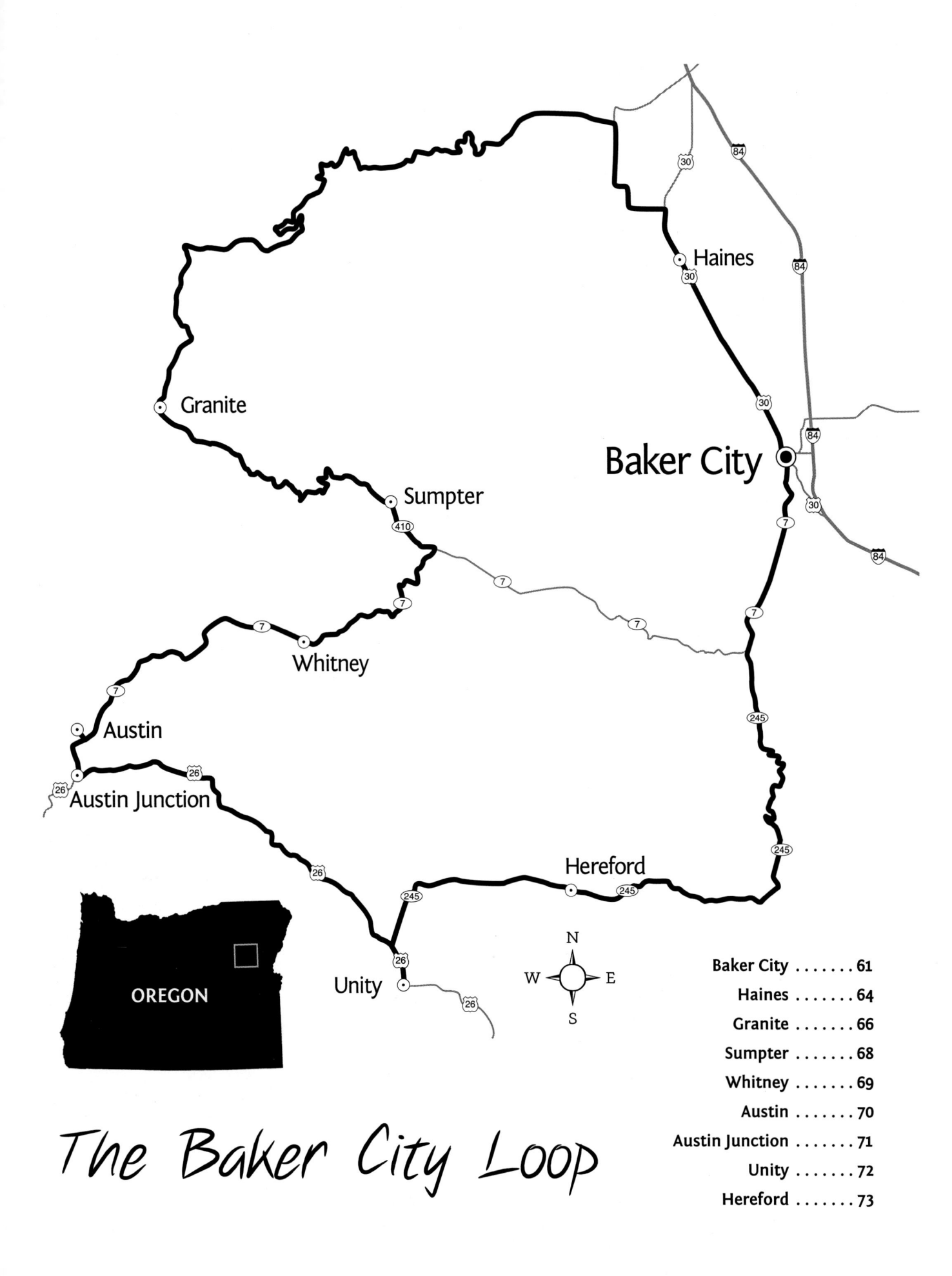

The Baker City Loop

Baker City	61
Haines	64
Granite	66
Sumpter	68
Whitney	69
Austin	70
Austin Junction	71
Unity	72
Hereford	73

Gold, Ghost Towns, and Granite
The Baker City Loop (166 miles)

The discovery of gold brought prosperity to many settlements along this route that begins and ends in Baker City, a community steeped in history. From Baker City, the route heads north to Haines, an important 19th century cow town that provided miners with necessary food and equipment.

From Haines, the route continues through the Elkhorn Mountains and the Anthony Lakes Ski Area toward Granite, named for an abundance of the hard, metamorphic rock. From Granite, the first of several ghost towns on this route, proceed to Sumpter and tour the gold dredge.

Take a ride on the Sumpter Valley Rail Road, visit a museum and pan for gold before heading to ghost towns of Bourne, Whitney, Tipton Station, Greenhorn and Austin.

Venture on to Bates, the ghost town under consideration to become a state park. From Bates, cross the Blue Mountain Pass to Unity, a small community that did not incorporate until 1972. Continue east toward Unity Lake and Hereford, and then return to Baker City, stopping en route at Griffin Creek where gold was first discovered in Baker County. Snow is common in May and not uncommon in late June, so inquire before heading from Haines to Granite and into the Anthony Lakes area.

the Blue Mountains as they rise near Haines

Baker City

Elevation: 3474 feet

Location:
44.46.312 N • 117.49.572 W

Services: gas, food, lodging, B&B, RV

Baker City was named to honor Edward Dickinson Baker, the first Oregonian to serve in the US Senate from 1860 to 1861. Shortly after Baker reached the rank of Major General, he was killed at the Battle of Balls Bluff during the Civil War. Baker was the only Senator ever killed in battle. Miners settled here in 1861, when gold was discovered in nearby Griffin Gulch, a few miles south of present day Baker City. Early structures built in the newly formed city included a house, saloon, hotel, blacksmith shop and quartz mill. Outfitting miners with food and supplies, gold mining and refining were its main economy. The town was platted in 1865 and the post office opened in 1866 under the name Baker City. This name was changed to Baker in 1911, and then reverted back to Baker City in 1989. Baker County was formed in 1862 when Wasco County was divided into smaller sections. Baker City became the county seat in 1868, was granted its charter in 1870, and incorporated in 1874. It was once the largest city between Salt Lake City and Portland. The railroad reached here in 1884. Baker City was known as the town without fire hydrants in 1888, when fire destroyed most of the wooden structures in the community. Agriculture, forestry, tourism and recreation are the biggest industries today.

Geiser Grand Hotel

Points of Interest

- **Baker City Hall** *(1655 1st)*
  Built in 1903 with marble stairs and granite steps. A copper roof makes it easy to see from the distance.

- **Telephone Exchange** *(1926 1st)*
  1889 telephone office.

- **Baker County Courthouse** *(3rd and Court)*
  Three stories with a clock tower.

- **Oregon Trail Regional Museum** *(2480 Grove)*
  Learn about rocks, pioneers, gold miners and Native Americans. Originally constructed as a natatorium in 1921.

- **Carnegie Library** *(2020 Auburn)*
  The 1909 library building houses the Crossroads Art Center.

- **Palmer Brothers Building** *(1801 Main)*
  Constructed in 1906.

- **Alfred Block** *(1806 Main)*
  In 1897, this was both a clothing and grocery store.

Carnegie Library

- **Bowen Building** (*1809 Main*)
  Built in 1886 and survived the devastating 1888 fire.

- **Bamberger Building** (*1813 Main*)
  Opened in 1888 and housed the Bedrock Democrat Newspaper.

- **Mint Building** (*1828 Main*)
  Built in 1889.

- **Fox Building** (*1830 Main*)
  Also built in 1889. Initially a cigar store.

Baker City Hall

- **The Elks Building** (*1910 Main*)
  Opened in 1897.

- **Alexander Building** (*1925 Main*)
  A men's clothing store in the 1890s.

- **Geiser Grand Hotel** (*1996 Main*)
  Three story hotel completed in 1889 and totally restored in 1997.

- **US Bank** (*2000 Main*)
  A chunk of gold, weighing over 80 ounces, is on display.

- **Lynndale Building** (*2020 Main*)
  A bar and cigar store in 1890.

- **Adler House** (*2305 Main*)
  Built in 1889.

- **Baer House** (*2333 Main*)
  Built in 1882. The 1889 Adler House is an exact twin.

- **Old Baker Hotel**
  (*Main and Auburn*)
  Ten-story, remodeled hotel built in 1929 is now home to businesses and condominiums.

- **Ira Bowen House**
  (*1701 Washington*)
  Built for the newspaper publisher in 1895.

- **Luther Ison House**
  (*1790 Washington*)
  Built as a private home in 1887 and housed The Bank of America since 1979. Judge Ison lived here only two years before he passed away in 1889.

- **St. Frances Catholic Church**
  (*2000 Church*)
  1908. Built with locally quarried stone.

- **Old City Park**
  (*Madison and Court*)
  In the center of the park is a 1906 monument, dedicated to the pioneers of the provisional government.

- **Baker City Chamber of Commerce** (*490 Campbell*)
  Helpful, courteous and knowledgeable employees.

St. Frances Catholic Church

- **Chinese Cemetery**
  (*Windmill Road*)
  Dates to 1892. Baker City had a large population of Chinese. Forty-six were originally buried in this cemetery.

- **Baker City National Historic Oregon Trail Interpretive Center** (*5 miles northeast of town on Highway 86*)
  Operated by the BLM and is one of the finest Oregon Trail Museums in the country. From the Interpretive Center, there is a short hike to view Oregon Trail wagon ruts.

Baer House

Baker City to Haines

Distance:
16.2 miles

Directions:
At the intersection of Main and Broadway in downtown Baker City, go west on Broadway.

Points En Route

(mileage from the intersection at Main and Broadway)

0.1 miles:
Turn right (north) on US 30, also called 10th St.

1.7 miles:
Turn left (west) on Pocahontas Road.

2.2 miles:
Miniature Shetland ponies.

4.7 miles:
Site of Pocahontas, an 1860s community with mining ties. The post office opened in 1862 and closed in 1864.

5.4 miles:
Pavement narrows.

6.1 miles:
The Pocahontas School.

8.6 miles:
Log cabin on left. Pocahontas Road veers right.

10.1 miles:
Abandoned, weathered house on Pine Creek Road. Pine Creek was a community in the 1860s that had its own post office until it consolidated with Pocahontas.

14.8 miles:
At stop sign, proceed straight.

15.0 miles:
At stop, go right (east) onto S. Rock Creek Lane.

15.1 miles:
Wind turbines on the distant hillsides.

16.2 miles:
Haines

the road to Haines

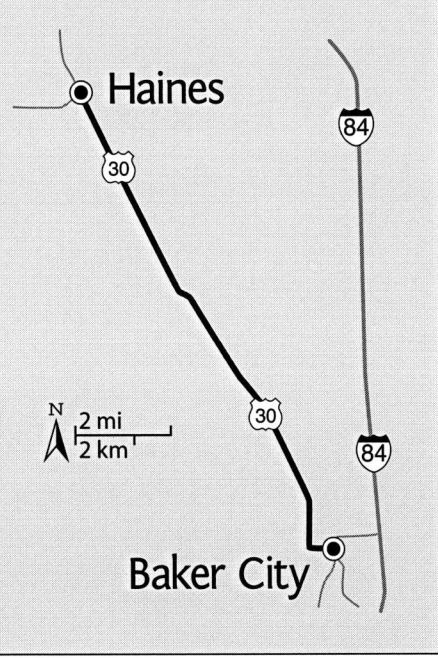

Haines

Elevation: 3333 feet

Location:
44.54.421 N • 117.56.242 W

Services: gas, food

Israel David Haines, for whom the town is named, owned over 1200 acres of farmland in the area. The post office opened in 1884, the same year the railroad came through town. Haines was platted in 1885 and incorporated in 1909. It was a major supplier of miner provisions and equipment, timber and agricultural products. Haines hosts an annual Fourth of July Celebration, complete with parade and rodeo. Five mountain peaks can be seen from the downtown, including Elkhorn Peak (8922 ft), Rock Creek Butte (9097 ft), Hunt Mountain (8232 ft), Red Mountain (8034 ft), and Twin Mountain (8920 ft). The city slogan, prominently displayed in the city park, reads, "Whiskey in the Water, Gold in the Streets!"

Downtown Haines

Points of Interest

- **Haines Mercantile and Store** *(4th and Front)*
  A café and grocery store built in 1905. Old mercantile items and photos of early Haines are displayed.

- **Chandler Cabin** *(4th and Front)*
  The 1861 cabin was moved to this site. The Mt. Carmel Letter Drop building and the old Hale pioneer Cabin are located nearby.

- **Haines City Park** *(4th and Front)*
  The park is located where cattleman loaded herds of cattle onto boxcars. From 1875-1884 over 100,000 head of cattle were sent to Wyoming and Montana.

- **Haines Methodist Church** *(4th and Robert)*
  Dates to the 1890s.

- **City Park**
  (extends from 2nd to 6th and Front)
  Many old buildings and displays, including a 1918 animal-watering trough. A covered walking bridge spans the creek.

- **Eastern Oregon Museum** *(610 3rd)*
  Open Thursdays through Mondays, May 15 to September 15. On site is the 100-year old Haines schoolhouse.

- **Bristow Building** *(3rd and Front)*
  Constructed in 1908. Houses the IOOF and Grocery Store.

- **Haines Railroad Depot** *(3rd and School)*
  The old depot, part of the museum, was constructed in 1885.

- **Elkhorn Grange Building #1908** *(3rd and Cole)*
  Built in the 1920s.

- **Haines Cemetery** *(15910 Neill-Peck Road)*
  Dates to 1895.

- **Rock Creek Cemetery** *(6 miles west of town at the foot of the Elkhorn Mountains)*
  One of the oldest cemeteries in Baker County, dating to 1862.

Chandler Cabin

Haines to Granite

Distance:
42.3 miles

Directions:
From 3rd and Front, go north on Front (Highway 30).

Points En Route

(mileage from 3rd and Front)

1.0 miles:
Log Cabin.

1.7 miles:
Turn left onto Haines Cemetery Road, heading west.

1.9 miles:
Pavement ends.

2.2 miles:
Railroad tracks.

2.8 miles:
Pavement returns.

3.0 miles:
At the intersection of Haines Cemetery Lane and Anthony Lakes Highway, turn left, heading west on Anthony Lakes Highway.

7.0 miles:
The Elkhorn Scenic Highway.

7.3 miles:
Road narrows and pavement is rough.

9.3 miles:
Elkhorn Ridge.

9.7 miles:
Entering Wallowa-Whitman National Forest.

13.1 miles:
Pullout and viewpoint.

17.7 miles:
Elkhorn Crest Trailhead.

17.8 miles:
Anthony Lake.

18.0 miles:
Anthony Lake Campground.

18.1 miles:
Mud Lake Campground.

18.2 miles:
Anthony Lake Ski Area.

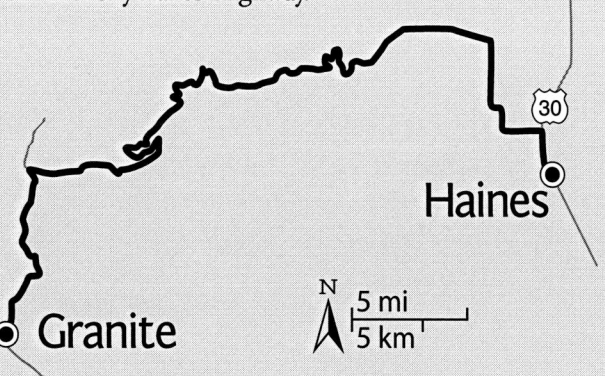

18.9 miles:
Access to Grande Ronde Lake.

19.6 miles:
Elkhorn Summit, 7392 feet.

21.0 miles:
At this point in July, 2008, the road was blocked with 7 feet of snow.

21.5 miles:
Viewpoint.

29.3 miles:
Peavy Cabin cccess.

33.9 miles:
Stop at the intersection of highway 73 and highway 52. Go left on highway 73 toward Granite. The North Fork John Day Campground is located at this intersection. An information kiosk provides information on the Blue Mountain Scenic Byway.

34.4 miles:
Crossing Onion Creek.

40.8 miles:
Mining tailings.

42.3 miles:
Granite

along the road to Granite

Granite

Elevation: 4750 feet

Location:
44.48.565 N • 118.25.062 W

Services: gas, food, lodging, RV

The gold strike community was first named Independence when gold was discovered on July 4, 1862. Due to the abundance of granite in the area and because another town in Polk County was already called Independence, the name was changed to Granite. The post office opened in 1878 and did not close until 1957 when the gold finally played out. At the time of incorporation in 1901, Granite had a drugstore, livery stable, dance hall, newspaper (the Granite Gem), blacksmith shop, two hotels, three stores and five saloons. At its peak, the population reached more than 5,000. Today the community has a population of fifteen. Telephone service did not reach Granite until the year 2000.

entrance to Granite

former schoolhouse

Points of Interest

- **Allen Hall** (*1529 Main*)
  Built as a Catholic Church in the 1930s.

- **Granite Drug Store** (*1530 Main*)
  Constructed in 1903.

- **Otis Ford Cabin** (*Main and Center*)
  Otis Ford came to Granite in the 1880s.

- **J.J. O'Dair Store** (*Main and Center*)
  General store, built in 1900.

- **Granite School** (*next to the O'Dair Store on Center*)
  Opened in 1913.

- **J.J. O'Dair Residence** (*Center*)
  The storeowner's home, located across the street from the Otis Ford Cabin.

- **Dance Hall** (*Main*)
  Located between the Stage Stop and the old drug store.

- **A.G. Tabor House** (*West*)
  Built in 1875. Tabor discovered the first gold in Granite.

- **Rose Starkey House** (*Grant*)
  Rose was badly burned trying to rescue a young boy from a fire that killed another young boy and eventually took her life.

- **Stage Stop** (*Grant and Main*)
  Built about 1898 and included a large reception area, dining room and four upstairs guest rooms.

- **Granite Cemetery** (*Tabor*)
  Scattered among the gravesites are many wooden markers. Rose Starkey is buried here.

- **China Walls Site** (*travel west on Main for 1.4 miles*)
  Rows of hand piled rocks remain at the site where Chinese worked the abandoned Granite mining claims.

Granite to Sumpter

Distance:
15.1 miles

Directions:
At the intersection of Center Street and Grant County Road #24 (also called Granite Hill Road), turn left and drive south toward Sumpter.

Points En Route

(mileage from the intersection of Center Street and Grant County Road #24)

The road follows Bull Run Creek. Mining tailings parallel the road for about five miles. Occasional green, lush meadows appear among lodge pole pine forests. Watch for mining claims and late spring and early fall accumulations of snow.

6.8 miles:
Forest practices information sign.

9.0 miles:
Summit of Blue Springs, 5864 feet.

9.0 miles:
Entering Baker County.

12.9 miles:
Chain removal area.

13.1 miles:
McCully Fork Campground. Primitive sites.

13.3 miles:
More mining tailings.

13.8 miles:
Leaving the Wallowa-Whitman National Forest.

15.1 miles:
Sumpter

15.3 miles:
Optional side trip to Bourne. Travel 5.8 miles up Cracker Creek Road to visit the ghost town of Bourne, elevation 5260 feet and location 44.49.372 W by 118.11.974 N. The road follows Cracker Creek, which was the original name of Bourne, renamed for US Senator Jonathan Bourne of Portland who had a keen interest in mining. The Bourne post office operated from 1895 until 1927. Heavy flooding damaged most of the businesses and homes in 1937. Only a few homes and several active mining claims remain in Bourne. The Cracker Creek Mining Company is a tourist attraction that teaches gold panning techniques. Evidence of mining is apparent most of the way to Bourne. At approximately one mile up Cracker Creek is the foundation of an old mining building that sits under two feet of water. Mining changed the course of the river that eventually consumed the old building.

abandoned cabin in Bourne

Sumpter

Elevation: 4388 feet

Location:
44.44.729 N • 118.12.314 W

Services: gas, food, B&B, lodging

Five men, looking for fertile land to farm, found gold here in 1862. Hailing from the South, the men named the new community Sumpter after their home in South Carolina. The town was platted in 1886; the railroad came to town in 1896 and incorporated in 1901. The big gold boom arrived in 1899 with the onset of hydraulic and hard rock mining. A brickyard, sawmill, smelter, electric lights, gravity flow water system, and streets paved with wooden planks turned the mining camp into a boomtown. At that time, Sumpter had a racetrack, brewery, dairy, cigar factory, hospital, China Town, an undertaker and coffin maker, sports teams, assayers, several livery stables, three blacksmith shops and sixteen saloons. In addition were a clothing store, opera house, newspaper office, telephone office, fire department, two banks, three general stores, four churches and five hotels. More than 3000 people and eighty-one businesses thrived here in 1901. By 1916 most of the gold had played out and the population dwindled. A major fire in August of 1917 destroyed the equivalent of twelve square blocks of businesses and homes. Gold dredges continued operating until 1924, when the behemoths fell silent. A new dredge, constructed in 1935, worked the creeks until WWII began, started again after the war and, finally, ceased all mining activity in 1954. Over $10 million in gold came from the Sumpter area. Sumpter is a collection of sleepy houses and quiet cabins, nestled among tall pines on gravel streets that come alive in winter and summer. Three small museums depict Sumpter in its heyday.

Sumpter Valley Railroad engine

Points of Interest

- **Sumpter Valley Gold Dredge State Heritage Area** *(Austin)*
  At no cost, people can enter the old dredge and see how it operated.

- **Sumpter Valley Railroad Depot** *(Austin)*
  The narrow gauge train now runs from the station to the rail museum, about 6 miles from town. It originally operated from 1890-1947.

- **Grocery and Museum** *(150 Main)*
  A convenience market with old Sumpter mining items displayed.

- **Dredge Superintendent's House** *(200 block of Main)*
  Residence of the dredge master when mining was in full swing.

- **Sumpter Dry Goods Store** *(231 Main)*
  Brick construction saved it from the 1917 fire.

- **Sumpter Bank Vault** *(next to the fire department on Main St)*
  The 1899 vault is all that remains of the Bank of Sumpter.

- **Mine Shaft** *(Main and High)*
  A hard rock mineshaft entrance.

- **Sumpter School** *(High and Hill)*
  Dates to 1918.

- **St. Brigids in the Pines** *(284 Auburn)*
  A community church, constructed after the 1917 fire.

- **Old Residence** *(275 Austin)*
  Beautiful stained glass windows in one of Sumpter's older homes.

- **Sumpter B & B** *(NE Columbia)*
  One of Sumpter's older homes.

the business end of the Sumpter Valley Gold Dredge

Sumpter to Whitney

Distance:
12.0 miles

Directions:
From the Cracker Creek Museum of Mining on Main Street, go southeast on Sumpter Highway toward Whitney.

Points En Route

(mileage from the Cracker Creek Museum)

0.1 miles:
Site of an old sawmill.

1.4 miles:
Sumpter Cemetery Road. The cemetery dates to the 1860s.

2.1 miles:
Large, old barn next to a small, quaint old home.

2.6 miles:
At the intersection of Sumpter Highway and Highway 7, turn right onto Highway 7, heading south toward John Day and Whitney.

3.0 miles:
Crossing the Powder River.

3.3 miles:
Entering the Wallowa-Whitman National Forest.

6.2 miles:
Summit.

8.2 miles:
Alpine meadow and snowmobile trails.

12.0 miles:
Whitney

Whitney

Elevation: 4200 feet

Location:
44.39.600 N • 118.17.482 W

Services: none

Not known as a gold mining community, Whitney's claim to fame was as a lumber town, where timbers were cut for mine shafts and dimension lumber was cut for the construction of miner's homes. The community was named for C.H. Whitney, early pioneer landowner and settler. Never a large community, Whitney had fewer than 100 people at its peak, and rapidly declined after the mill burned in 1918. The train trestle, removed in 1915 because it was so dangerous, was the second highest in the world. The Whitney post office operated from 1901 to 1943. The railroad came to town in 1901 and was abandoned by 1947. Most of the old buildings stand on private property. Remains of the mill include the log pond and scattered pieces of rusting machinery.

Point of Interest

- **Whitney Road**
  Drive along Whitney Road to view a series of old houses and barns.

barn between Sumpter and Whitney

Whitney to Austin

Distance:
14.0 miles

Directions:
From the intersection of Whitney Road and Highway 7, turn left, heading southwest on Highway 7.

Points En Route

(mileage from the intersection of Whitney Road and Highway 7)

The highway follows the North Fork of the Burnt River.

2.5 miles:
Picturesque, abandoned cabins and outbuildings.

4.3 miles:
Crossing the Burnt River.

7.2 miles:
Tipton Station Historical Marker. The Tipton post office opened in 1904 and closed in 1906. Tipton was located at the highest point on the Sumpter Valley Railway and was an important train station in the Blue Mountains.

7.3 miles:
Greenhorn Road. (A seven-mile side-trip on a gravel road) Greenhorn, incorporated in 1903, is located at the 6300-foot level, the highest elevation of any Oregon city. After almost forty years of mining, the Greenhorn post office opened in 1902. The office closed soon after in 1919. The Greenhorn Jail was moved to Canyon City, where it stands today at the Grant County Museum. Only a few other buildings still exist, with little to remind us of the 2000 residents that once lived here.

7.8 miles:
Entering Grant County.

13.3 miles:
Turn right onto Austin Road (Grant County Road 20A).

14.0 miles:
Austin

Austin

Elevation: 4115 feet

Location:
44.36.207 N • 118.29.838 W

Services: none

Austin is located nineteen miles northeast of Prairie City and was the terminus of the Sumpter Valley Railroad. Austin was a supply depot on the railroad, abandoned when the mines in the area closed. At one time it had a population of over 500, mostly workers and families who provided services for the miners, the mines and the mining communities. Austin received its name from Mr. and Mrs. Minot Austin, the owners of the stagecoach way station and hotel when the post office opened in 1888. The hotel remained open until the late 1930s. During its heyday, Austin boasted several doctors, lawyers and three sawmills. Today, only a few homes line a forgotten, dead end street.

home in Austin

Austin to Austin Junction

Distance:
2.6 miles

Directions:
From the Austin sign, return on Austin Road to Highway 7.

Points En Route

(mileage from the Austin, OR city sign)

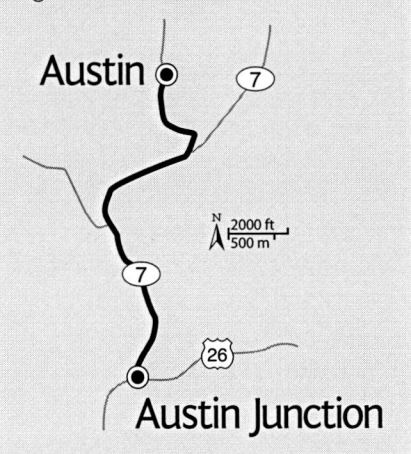

0.7 miles:
At the intersection of Austin Road and Highway 7, go right, heading west on Highway 7 toward Bates.

1.6 miles:
Bates. The community was named for Paul C. Bates, an insurance agent from Portland who helped negotiate the purchase of timberland when the Oregon Lumber Company first ventured into the wood product business. The state is negotiating with the community to make it a state park.

2.6 miles:
Austin Junction

Austin Junction

Elevation: 4264 feet

Location:
44.34.414 N • 118.00.152 W

Services: gas, food

Austin Junction is located at the intersection of Highway 7 and Highway 26.

Austin House

the road to Unity

Austin Junction to Unity

Distance:
19.5 miles

Directions:
From the Austin Country Store, go left, heading east, on Highway 26 toward Unity.

Points En Route

(mileage from the Austin Country Store)

0.2 miles:
Department of Austin Transportation Maintenance Station.

4.8 miles:
Picturesque barn and house facing the old highway.

8.3 miles:
Summit of Blue Mountain Pass, 5109 feet.

8.6 miles:
Entering Baker County.

9.0 miles:
Wallowa-Whitman National Forest Campground. Primitive facilities.

10.9 miles:
Yellow Pine Campground. Primitive facilities.

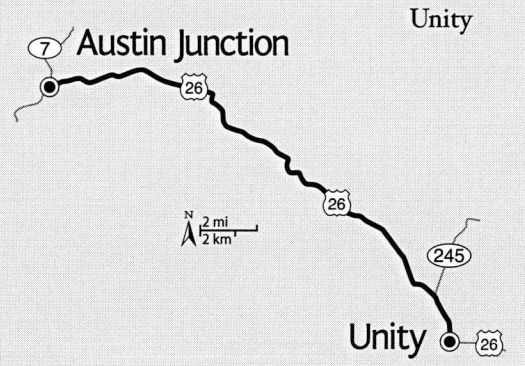

11.5 miles:
Wetmore Campground.

11.9 miles:
A second entrance to the Wetmore Campground.

13.0 miles:
Leaving Wallowa-Whitman National Forest.

14.9 miles:
Uniquely constructed fence corners.

15.5 miles:
Remains of a settlement and an old root cellar.

16.7 miles:
Unity Cemetery Road. The cemetery dates to the 1880s.

16.9 miles:
Burnt River Community Church.

17.0 miles:
Abandoned shack and outbuildings.

18.4 miles:
Intersection with Highway 26 and Highway 245. Go right on Highway 26 toward Unity.

19.5 miles:
Unity

Unity

Elevation: 4029 feet

Location:
44.49.372 N • 118.11.974 W

Services: gas, food, lodging, RV

In 1861, Robert Murray settled in this area. The name comes from the unity that the local farmers enjoyed in their valley. The post office opened in 1891. This small community of 110 was not incorporated until 1972.

Points of Interest

- **Statton's Store** *(101 Main)*
  A second grocery store, now closed.

- **Old Ice Cream Store** *(110 Main)*
  Once sold groceries and ice cream. Built with a unique porch.

- **Wallowa-Whitman Ranger Station** *(214 Main)*
  The station administers over 190,000 acres.

- **El Dorado Ditch**
  A ditch dug by Chinese laborers to channel water for hydraulic mining in the Sumpter Valley. The ditch is visible behind the community center.

- **Burnt River Schools**
  The current hub of community activity.

Statton's Store

Hereford Union High School

Hereford

Elevation: 3667 feet

Location:
44.29.910 N • 118.02.252 W

Services: none

Hereford was named when a Hereford steer was led through town about the time the community was forming. Ranching and farming are the main industries.

barn near Unity

Unity to Hereford

Distance:
11.5 miles

Directions:
At the Burnt River School, go west on Highway 26 toward the intersection of Highways 26 and 245.

Points En Route

(mileage from Burnt River School)

0.6 miles:
Old millpond.

1.5 miles:
At the intersection of Highways 26 and 245, go right onto Highway 245, toward Hereford and Baker City.

3.8 miles:
St. Joseph Catholic Church.

3.9 miles:
Unity Lake State Park.

4.6 miles:
Unity Dam, constructed in 1937.

5.2 miles:
Road parallels the Burnt River.

5.8 miles:
Interesting rock outcroppings.

6.8 miles:
Eldred Ranch.

9.9 miles:
Old windmill and ranch. The road winds through a valley, unspoiled and quiet.

11.5 miles:
Hereford

Hereford to Baker City

Distance:
32.4 miles

Directions:
From Hereford School, continue east on Highway 245 toward Salisbury and Baker City.

Points En Route

(mileage from Hereford Union Schools)

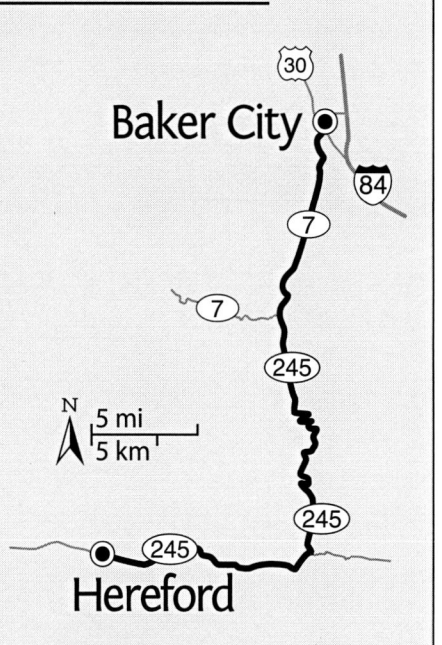

0.4 miles:
The 1884 Trimble Land and Cattle Company.

4.1 miles:
Perhaps a former community.

4.4 miles:
Rustic fencing.

6.6 miles:
Bald Mountain Mining Company Operations.

9.2 miles:
Dilapidated shack.

10.0 miles:
Old outbuildings.

10.2 miles:
Keep left, heading toward Baker City.

16.3 miles:
Beautiful vistas.

17.9 miles:
Dooley Mountain Summit. Snow capped mountains are visible in the distance.

22.3 miles:
Leaving the Wallowa-Whitman National Forest. Old outbuildings.

24.2 miles:
Topography changes to sagebrush and small pines.

25.3 miles:
Intersection and side trip to Salisbury. Turn left and drive 1.6 miles. An old cabin and homestead remain at the site of Salisbury. The Salisbury post office opened in 1894 and closed in 1896. The community was named after the first postmaster, Francis Salisbury. Return to this intersection and continue the route toward Baker City.

26.9 miles:
Old Auburn Lane, a wildlife viewing area and alternate route to Auburn.

31.8 miles:
Griffin Gulch, where gold was first discovered in Baker City. A short side trip.

32.4 miles:
Baker City

old outbuildings

a view down the valley

74

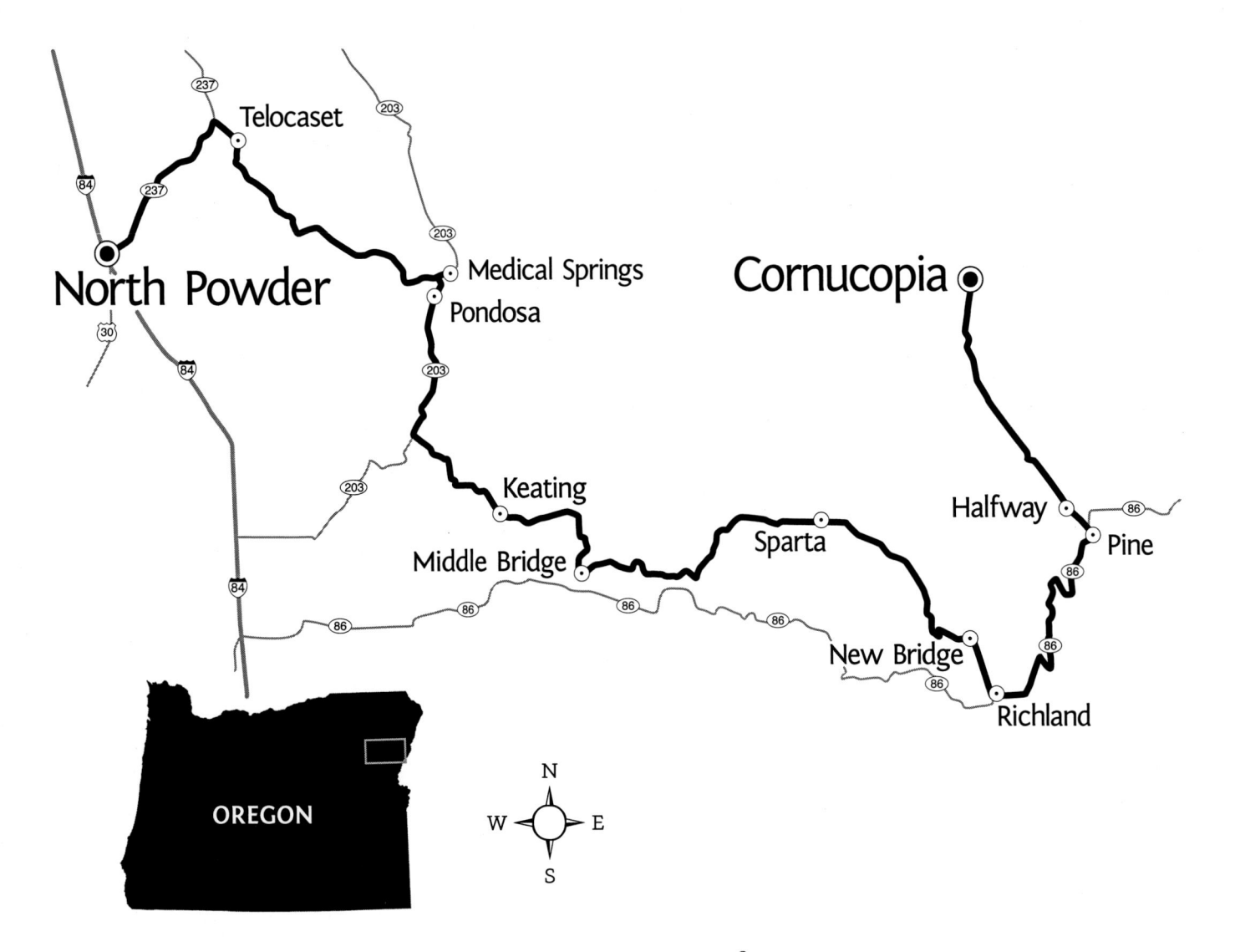

North Powder to Cornucopia

North Powder 77
Telocaset 78
Medical Springs 79
Pondosa 80
Keating 81
Middle Bridge 82
Sparta 83
New Bridge 84
Richland 85
Pine 86
Halfway 87
Cornucopia 89

From the Geographic Center of the US to a Horn of Plenty

North Powder to Cornucopia (89 miles)

Spectacular scenery, ghost haunts and mining history can all be experienced on this route that begins at Exit 285 on I-84 near North Powder, a community settled in the 1860s. From there, the route continues to Telocaset, the geographic center of the United States and then to Medical Lake, where pioneers bathed in the naturally heated sulfur water.

A company store still stands in Pondosa, a mill town en route to Keating, a small agricultural community built around the school. Continue through Middle Bridge to Sparta, a ghost town that once flourished when gold was discovered there in 1863.

Cross Eagle Creek at New Bridge, then drive on to Richland, nestled in the fertile soils of the Eagle Valley. Follow highway 86 to Halfway, where ghosts allegedly haunt the upstairs of a local tavern. End the trip at the gold mines of Cornucopia, or experience Hells Canyon, the deepest in the United States, on two final, optional routes that originate in Halfway.

wind turbines near Telocaset

North Powder

Elevation: 3261 feet

Location:
45.02.481 N • 117.55.533 W

Services: gas, food

North Powder is a small town with fewer than 500 residents. It was named after the North Powder River, a tributary of the Powder River. A stage station operated near this site on the Oregon Trail in 1862 and the North Powder post office opened in 1866. The town had a newspaper, school, three churches and twelve businesses when it incorporated in 1902. An Ice Plant, in operation from 1897 to 1937, provided ice for rail cars delivering produce to Portland markets. A history marker indicates the site where, in 1811, Madame Dorian gave birth to the first white child born west of the Rockies. She is buried in St. Louis, near Gervais, in Marion County.

IOOF Building

Points of Interest

- **IOOF Building** *(165 E)*
  Built in 1889, now an antique store.

- **Baker Mill and Grain**
  (behind the IOOF building)
  Built in the 1880s.

- **A.B. Hudelson and Son Dry Goods and Grocery** *(2nd and E)*
  Dates to 1900.

- **Wolf Creek Grange Hall #596** *(215 E)*
  An old advertising curtain hangs on the wall inside the building.

- **North Powder Library** *(290 E)*
  Housed in the original 1930s fire hall. Many old photos are on display here.

- **North Powder City Park**
  (next to the Library on E)
  Gazebo and picnic area. A water tower dwarfs the park grounds. Three unknown concrete structures are located below the storage tank.

- **United Methodist Church** *(390 E)*
  A beautiful, old building, built in 1907.

- **North Powder School** *(333 G)*
  Two-story construction, built in 1911.

- **City Hall** *(635 3rd)*
  Over 100 years old.

Baker Mill and Grain

A.B. Hudelson and Son Dry Goods and Grocery

North Powder to Telocaset

Distance:
7.4 miles

Directions:
From the intersection of 2nd and E, go northeast on 2nd toward Telocaset.

Points En Route

(mileage from the intersection at 2nd and E)

0.4 miles:
North Powder Lumber Company.

0.5 miles:
North Powder Cemetery, dates to the 1870s.

1.1 miles:
Wind turbines on the hillside.

2.6 miles:
Row of old cottonwood trees, planted as a wind block.

3.1 miles:
Historical Marker. Marie Dorion gave birth to her third child here in 1811. It was the first white child born west of the Mississippi River. Dorion died in St. Louis, Oregon, in 1850. A stage stop was built near here in 1862.

6.9 miles:
Turn right on Telocaset Lane.

7.4 miles:
Telocaset

Telocaset

Elevation: 3446 feet

Location:
45.10.111 N • 117.82.528 W

Services: none

Located at the intersection of Telocaset Road and Railroad Lane, this former community was the site of the Antelope Stage Station. Telocaset is Nez Perce for 'thing at the top.' The post office opened in 1885. Telocaset is the geographic center of the United States and was established on an old toll road that ran from Boise to Portland.

wind turbines and old shed

the road to Telocaset

78

Telocaset to Medical Springs

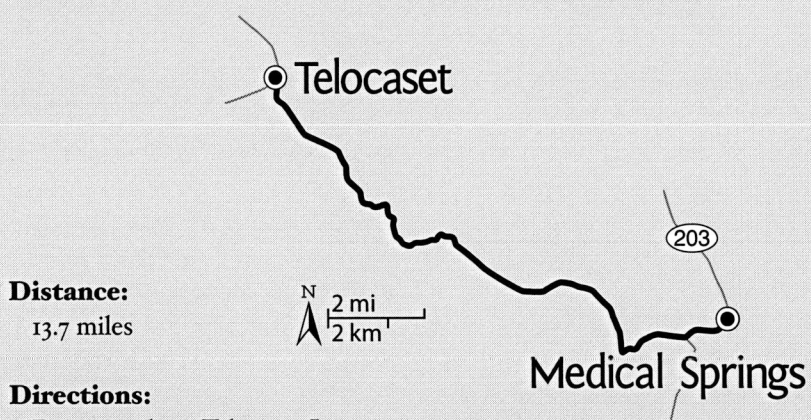

Distance: 13.7 miles

Directions: Drive south on Telocaset Lane.

Points En Route

(mileage from the intersection of Telocaset Lane and the RR tracks)

The road is well-maintained dirt and gravel.

1.3 miles: Go left, remaining on Telocaset Lane. Follow the Grande Tour Scenic Route.

1.5 miles: Attractive, old farm with views of the Blue Mountains, wind turbines, pastureland, and sagebrush-covered, rolling hills.

4.3 miles: View of Horse Thief Reservoir.

5.5 miles: Optional 1.6 mile side trip to the reservoir. Turn right onto Thief Valley Reservoir Road. Return to Telocaset Lane.

7.1 miles: Columnar Basalt formations.

8.6 miles: Abandoned farm.

12.8 miles: At stop sign, go left on Highway 203 toward Medical Springs. Pavement returns and follows the Grand Tour Scenic Route.

13.7 Medical Springs

Medical Springs

Elevation: 3387 feet

Location: 45.01.722 N • 117.62.751 W

Services: food

Medical Springs is mentioned frequently in pioneer journals and was named for the hot, mineral water pools with their unmistakable sulfur scent. Dunham and Artemisia Wright homesteaded the area in the late 1800s and fifth generation descendants live on and farm the property. A destination hotel and pool operated in the 1930s and 1940s.

Points of Interest

- **Old Medical Springs Pool**
  (corner Highway 203 and Eagle Creek Drive)
  Pioneers frequently bathed in the naturally heated waters. In 1929, the original bathhouse was struck by lightning and destroyed.

- **Medical Springs Hotel**
  (at intersection)
  The first hotel burned in the 1880s. The second, built in 1918, is now apartments.

- **Ox Bow Guest Ranch**
  (next to the Medical Springs Hotel)
  Private residence of the great, great granddaughter of Dunham Wright.

Old Medical Springs Pool

Pondosa

Elevation: 3260 feet

Location:
45.02.880 N • 117.38.310 W

Services: food

Pondosa, a lumber town, was named for the Ponderosa pine trees that grow in the region. A post office opened in 1927. The local mill, that cut logs into dimension lumber in its heyday, closed in the late 1950s and was razed shortly thereafter. At one time, Pondosa was home to more than 500 people and seventy houses. Unfortunately, a 1950s fire claimed most of the older businesses and residences as well. Originally a boarding hotel, the Pondosa Store survived the fire and now provides food and drink to travelers. Pictures of Pondosa, before the fire, are displayed in the store.

Points of Interest

- **Pondosa Store**
  Open since the 1920s.

- **Lumber Headquarters Vault**
  A vault, that stands near the decked foundation of the company headquarters building, is all that remains of the mill.

- **Railroad Worker Quarters**
  (behind the decked foundation)
  Employees of the railroad were housed in this dormitory-like structure.

- **School Bell Tower**
  The cupola is all that is left of the 1927 school.

Medical Springs to Pondosa

Distance:
1.1 miles

Directions:
From the Medical Springs pool, return west on Highway 203.

Points En Route

(mileage from the pool)

0.8 miles:
Keep left on Highway 203

1.1 miles:
Pondosa

Pondosa Store

Lumber Headquarters Vault

Pondosa to Keating

Distance:
11.9 miles

Directions:
Continue south on Highway 203.

Points En Route

(mileage from the Pondosa Store)

1.0 miles:
Entering Baker County.

1.7 miles:
Crossing Big Creek.

6.3 miles:
Turn left onto Miles Bridge Road.

7.1 miles:
Medical Springs Grange #427, with his/her outhouses.

9.9 miles:
Pavement ends.

10.7 miles:
Abandoned farm.

11.8 miles:
Pavement returns.

11.9 miles:
Keating

Keating

Elevation: 3313 feet

Location:
44.52.433 N • 117.35.250 W

Services: none

The first settler in the area was an English sailor, Tom Keating, for whom the community was named. The post office opened in the early 1880s. The agricultural community consists of a few homes and a new school.

Points of Interest

- **Former Keating Store**
  Long vacant, built in the early 1900s.

Former Keating Store

Keating to Middle Bridge

Distance:
5.9 miles

Directions:
From the Keating Store, go east on Keating Grange Lane.

Points En Route

(mileage from the store)

0.2 miles:
Pavement ends.

0.3 miles:
Tucker Creek Hunting Reserve.

1.3 miles:
View of the Wallowa Mountains in the distance.

3.2 miles:
At the 'Y,' keep right, staying on Keating Grange Lane.

4.1 miles:
Rural Fire Station.

4.8 miles:
Stay right on Keating Grange Lane.

5.9 miles:
Middle Bridge

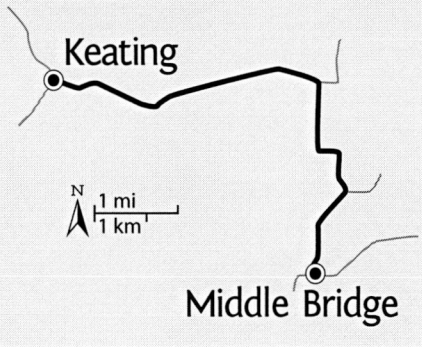

Middle Bridge

Elevation: 3541 feet

Location:
44.84.028 N • 117.52.417 W

Services: none

Middle Bridge was named for its location where one of three bridges spans the Powder River. The two-story home at this intersection was the 1880s stage stop and is home to "Poe," a rescued raven.

Points of Interest

- **Stage Stop**
  (now a private residence)
  Constructed in the 1880s and operational for about ten years.

"Poe" the rescued raven

the road to Middle Bridge

82

Middle Bridge to Sparta

Distance:
13.9 miles

Directions:
Turn left onto Middle Bridge Loop Road. Go east toward Sparta.

Points En Route

(mileage from the intersection of Keating Lane and Middle Bridge Loop Road)

4.1 miles:
Turn left onto Sparta Road. Pavement ends. The road affords expansive views of the valley below.

7.9 miles:
Old cabin adjacent to a newer home.

10.1 miles:
Stone house.

10.3 miles:
Summit. Beautiful views of the Wallowa Mountains.

11.0 miles:
Continue straight on Sparta Road.

11.1 miles:
Small settlement.

12.2 miles:
Gem Mine Road.

13.2 miles:
Abandoned cabin (to the right amid brush).

13.8 miles:
Log cabin (one of the remaining Sparta homes).

13.9 miles:
Sparta

Sparta

Elevation: 4090 feet

Location:
44.87.111 N • 117.32.306 W

Services: none

Sparta has had more names than the number of current residents. It was first named Koster, after Tom Koster who discovered gold here in 1863. It was subsequently changed to Eagle City, and then to Gem after the hard rock mine that was located here. It became Sparta in 1872, named by William Packwood who came from Sparta, Illinois. Packwood was the great-grandfather of former Senator Bob Packwood. Supposedly, three men, who died in a gunfight in 1869, are buried on "Boot Hill," located on a small rise south of town. At one time, Sparta had a population of over 5,000.

Points of Interest

- **Sparta Store**
  1878 stone construction.

- **Sparta Cemetery**
  Dates to about 1870 and is located on private property.

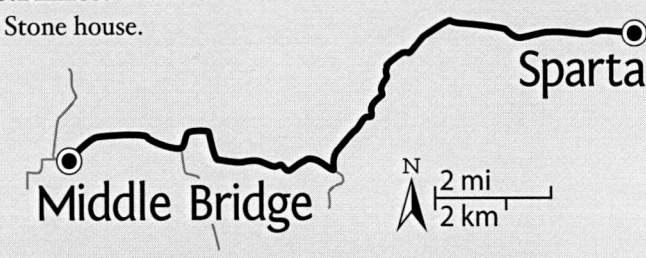

stone house

Sparta Store

Sparta to New Bridge

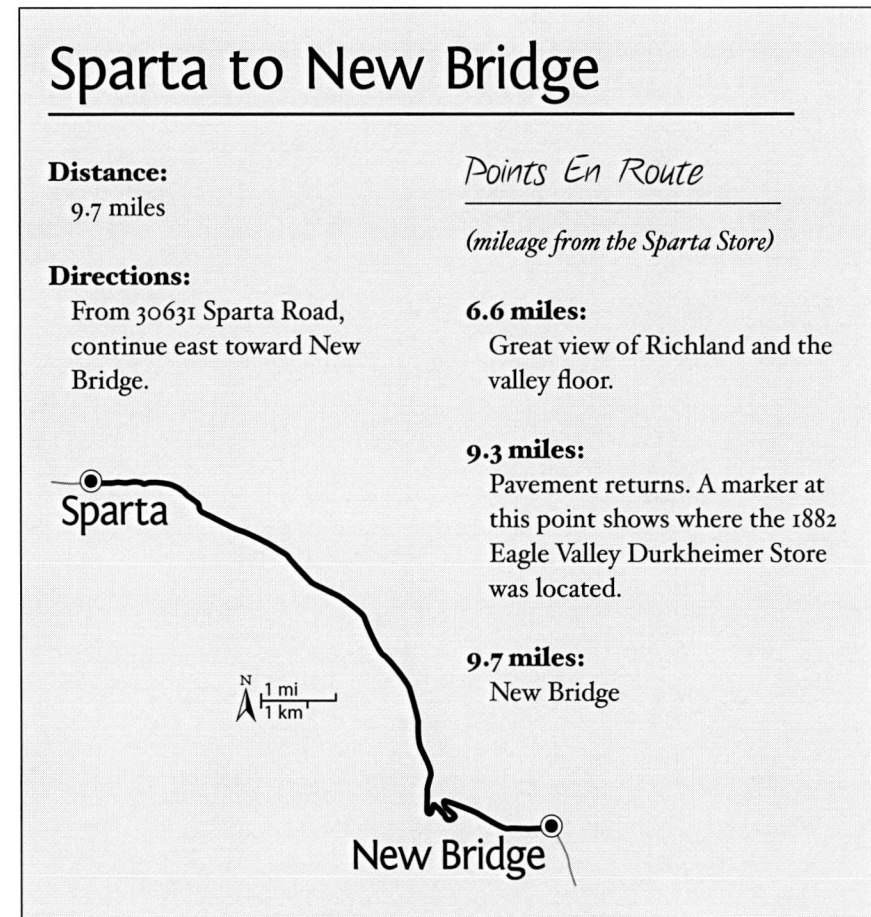

Distance:
9.7 miles

Directions:
From 30631 Sparta Road, continue east toward New Bridge.

Points En Route

(mileage from the Sparta Store)

6.6 miles:
Great view of Richland and the valley floor.

9.3 miles:
Pavement returns. A marker at this point shows where the 1882 Eagle Valley Durkheimer Store was located.

9.7 miles:
New Bridge

New Bridge

Elevation: 2362 feet

Location:
44.48.042 N • 117.11.069 W

Services: none

New Bridge is the site of an important pioneer bridge that spanned Eagle Creek. The post office opened in 1878 and did not close until 1967. A "new bridge" was later constructed, giving the community its name. New Bridge is a quaint community that played a vital role in getting supplies to miners in Sparta.

Points of Interest

- **New Bridge Grange**
  (43108 Main)
  The hall is used frequently and bingo is played the first Monday of every month.

- **Nazarene Church**
  (Main, next to the grange)
  Built in the early 1900s.

Nazarene Church

view along the road to New Bridge

New Bridge to Richland

Distance:
2.3 miles

Directions:
From the intersection of Newbridge Road and 2nd Street, go southeast on Newbridge Road toward Richland.

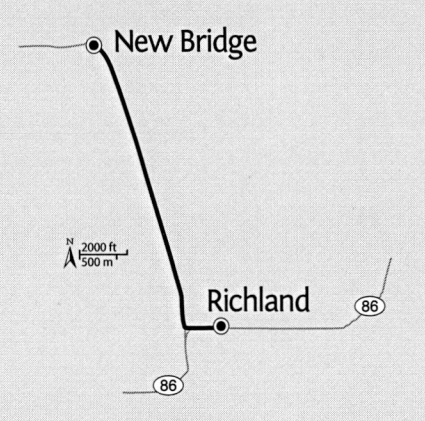

Points En Route

(mileage from the intersection)

0.5 miles:
Old farmhouse with red brick outbuildings.

1.2 miles:
Attractive, older farmhouse.

1.9 miles:
Grand, old farmhouse.

2.2 miles:
Turn left onto Highway 86. Eagle Valley Community Park.

2.3 miles:
Richland

Richland

Elevation: 2224 feet

Location:
44.46.035 N • 117.10.159 W

Services: gas, food, lodging, RV

Richland, a community of less than 200 inhabitants, received its name from the rich, fertile soil of the region. The post office opened in 1897 and the city incorporated in 1917. Agriculture continues to be the main economy.

Points of Interest:

- **General Store** *(100 Main)*
  Opened in the 1900s.

- **JD's Mercantile** *(102 Main)*
  Opened as the drug store about 1903.

- **Richland Bank** *(110 Main)*
  The empty, concrete block structure was constructed in 1910.

- **Longbranch Restaurant** *(114 Main)*
  Initially opened as the post office.

- **Fraternal Lodge** *(221 1st)*
  Circa 1907.

- **Richland Christian Church** *(117 2nd)*
  Dates to the early 1900s.

- **Richland United Methodist Church** *(226 2nd)*
  Built in 1906 with beautiful stained glass windows.

Richland United Methodist Church

Richland Bank

Richland to Pine

Distance:
10.8 miles

Directions:
From the corner of Main and Moody, go east on Highway 86.

Points En Route

(mileage from the intersection of Main and Moody)

0.0 miles:
Eagle Valley RV Park.

0.6 miles:
Follow Highway 86 left toward Hells Canyon (heading north).

2.8 miles:
Brownlee Reservoir is seen to the right.

6.2 miles:
Summit, 3353 feet.

6.9 miles:
Views of Halfway on the valley floor.

10.6 miles:
Veer right onto Sawmill Cutoff Lane.

10.6 miles:
Hells Canyon Information Wayside.

10.8 miles:
Pine

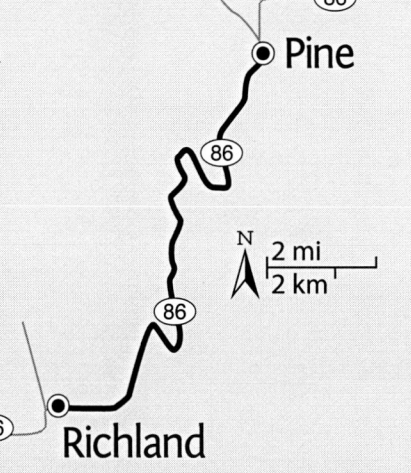

Pine

Elevation: 2489 feet

Location:
44.51.634 N • 117.05.011 W

Services: none

Pine, named for indigenous trees in the area, was first settled in the early 1870s. The post office opened in 1878 under the name of Pine Valley and was shortened to Pine in 1892. The first school was constructed in 1892 and was replaced by the current building.

Points of Interest:

- **Pine School**
  1912.

- **Pine General Store**
  An old gas pump stands sentinel.

- **Pine Ranger Station**
  Located at the intersection of Sawmill Cut-off road and Pine Town Road.

Pine School

Pine General Store

86

Pine to Halfway

Distance:
1.3 miles

Directions:
From the Sawmill Cut-off Road and Pine Town Lane intersection, go northwest toward Halfway.

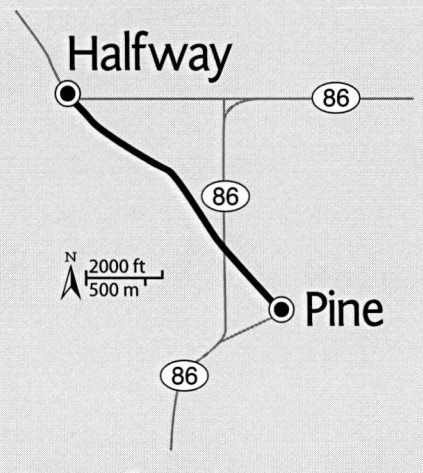

Points En Route

(mileage from the Pine Ranger Station)

0.4 miles:
Intersection with Highway 86. Continue straight.

0.9 miles:
VFW Hall.

1.1 miles:
Site of the first cabin in Halfway (1860 Charles L. Free home). Fairgrounds are visible from this site.

1.3 miles:
Halfway

Halfway

Elevation: 2625 feet

Location:
44.52.512 N • 117.06.450 W

Services: gas, food, lodging, RV

Halfway was said to be located halfway between the town of Pine and the gold mines of Cornucopia, hence, its name. Before settlers came, the area was an important Nez Perce, Shoshone, Umatilla and Snake Indian hunting ground. Benjamin Bonneville first mapped the area in the 1830s and the area was settled in the 1860s. The first public school house was constructed about 1882, the pioneer smokehouse in 1885 and the jail in 1909. The post office opened in 1887 and the town incorporated in 1909. The first concrete sidewalks were poured on September 24, 1928. In 1999, for a large amount of money, the name of the community was changed to Half.com. Halfway is less than a 30-minute drive to the Idaho border. The popular 1960s movie, *Paint Your Wagon*, was filmed here.

Points of Interest:

- **Stockman Bar** *(146 Main)*
  Ghosts of individuals, who died in the upstairs rooms, allegedly haunt the old bar.

- **Halfway Cemetery** *(Record Street and Slaughterhouse Road)*
  Dates to 1905.

- **Pine Valley Museum** *(155A Record)*
  Next to City Hall.

- **Site of Old Livery Stable** *(145 Record)*
  The building at 135 Record was part of the old stable.

- **Presbyterian Church** *(Church and Gover)*
  Established in 1905.

- **Old Church**
  Dates to 1891.

- **Old Store** *(151 Main)*
  Early 1900s.

- **Halfway Bank** *(Gover and Main)*
  The IOOF Hall is upstairs in this 1910 building.

- **Victorian House** *(112 Record)*
  One of the nicest in Halfway.

- **Halfway Liquor Store** *(143 Main)*
  Formerly the Halfway Hotel.

old store

Halfway to Cornucopia

Distance:
10.5 miles

Directions:
From the intersection of N. Main and E. Record Street near the Old Pine Market, go north on N. Main toward Cornucopia.

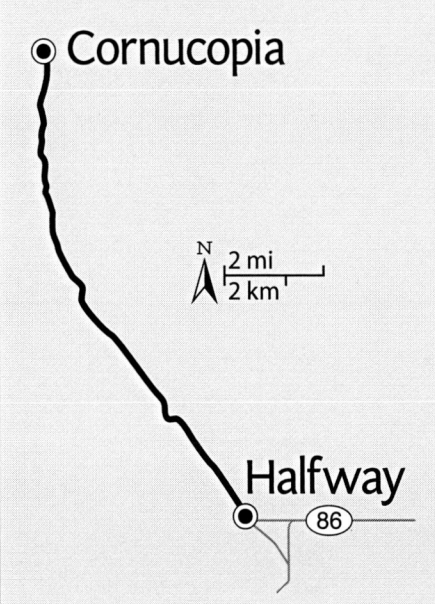

Points En Route

(mileage from the Old Pine Market)

2.5 miles:
Jimtown. Once known as Langrell, Jimtown was named for James Chandler who operated a general store at this location in 1910. Chandler purchased the 1904 store from Richard Langrell.

4.9 miles:
Carson. This former community was named for Thomas Corson (pronounced "Carson"), who settled here in 1870. The post office opened in 1893 and closed in 1952.

5.7 miles:
Pavement ends.

10.5 miles:
Cornucopia

Jimtown

nice house in Carson

along the road to Cornucopia

88

Cornucopia

Elevation: 4704 feet

Location:
45.00.591 N•117.15.255 W

Services: none

Cornucopia comes from the Latin word meaning 'horn of plenty.' Gold was discovered here in 1884 and the rich deposits were mined until the 1940s. Large quantities of silver and copper were also removed from the mines. The post office opened in 1885 and was discontinued following WWII. Harsh winters have taken a toll on the old buildings of this once prosperous, bustling community. Only a few remain standing. Mount Cornucopia is 8650 feet high.

abandoned buidling

cabin

looking into Cornucopia

Optional drive: Halfway to Hell's Canyon

Distance:
Alternate Route A – 16.5 miles
Alternate Route B – 30.1 miles:

Directions:
From the intersection of North Main and East Record, go east toward Oxbow and Hell's Canyon Dam. Follow signs to Highway 86.

Points En Route

(mileage from the Old Pine Market)

0.1 miles:
Pine Haven Cemetery, which dates to 1880.

0.8 miles:
Stop sign. Continue east on Highway 86.

4.5 miles:
Old farmhouse.

9.7 miles:
Intersection of Highway 86 and Highway 39.

Choose Alternate A or B.

Alternate A

Go right on Highway 86 to Copperfield and Oxbow Dam. The highway follows Pine Creek to the Snake River.

14.2 miles:
Hillside Bed and Breakfast.

14.3 miles:
Pine Creek. Gas, food, lodging and RV.

16.5 miles:
Intersection.

Go left to Homestead (3.9 miles) and Hell's Canyon Dam (23 miles). About halfway between Copperfield and Homestead is the 1902 Copperfield-Homestead Cemetery. Go right to Oxbow Dam (2 miles) and Brownlee Dam (12 miles). The area just north of Oxbow was Copperfield. The Copperfield post office opened in 1899 and abruptly closed in 1901. The post office reopened in 1907 when the railroad began tunneling near here. Lawlessness prevailed and in 1914, Governor Oswald West, in an effort to clean up the town, declared Marshall Law on Copperfield, closing all the saloons and seizing all gambling devices and weapons. A fire in 1915 destroyed most of the mining community. By 1927, two more fires had wiped out remaining buildings.

Alternate B

Go left onto Highway 39 toward Hell's Canyon Overlook. Hell's Canyon is the deepest canyon in North America, surpassing Arizona's Grand Canyon.

16.1 miles:
North Pine picnic area.

18.9 miles:
Lake Fork Forest Camp.

29.3 miles:
Turn right, heading northeast toward the overlook.

30.1 miles:
Hell's Canyon Overlook. Unbelievable views. Hell's Canyon is 7993 feet deep and ten miles across at its widest point.

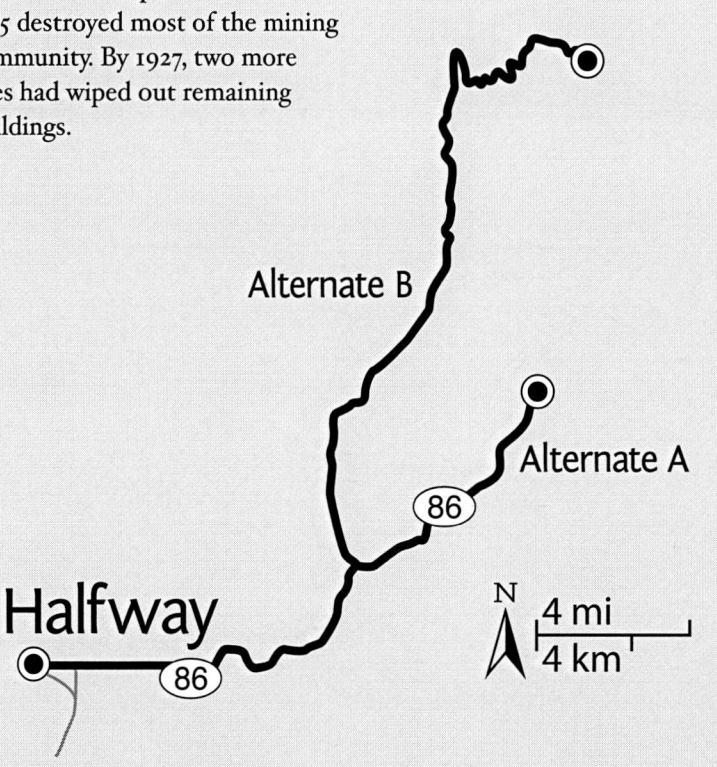

90

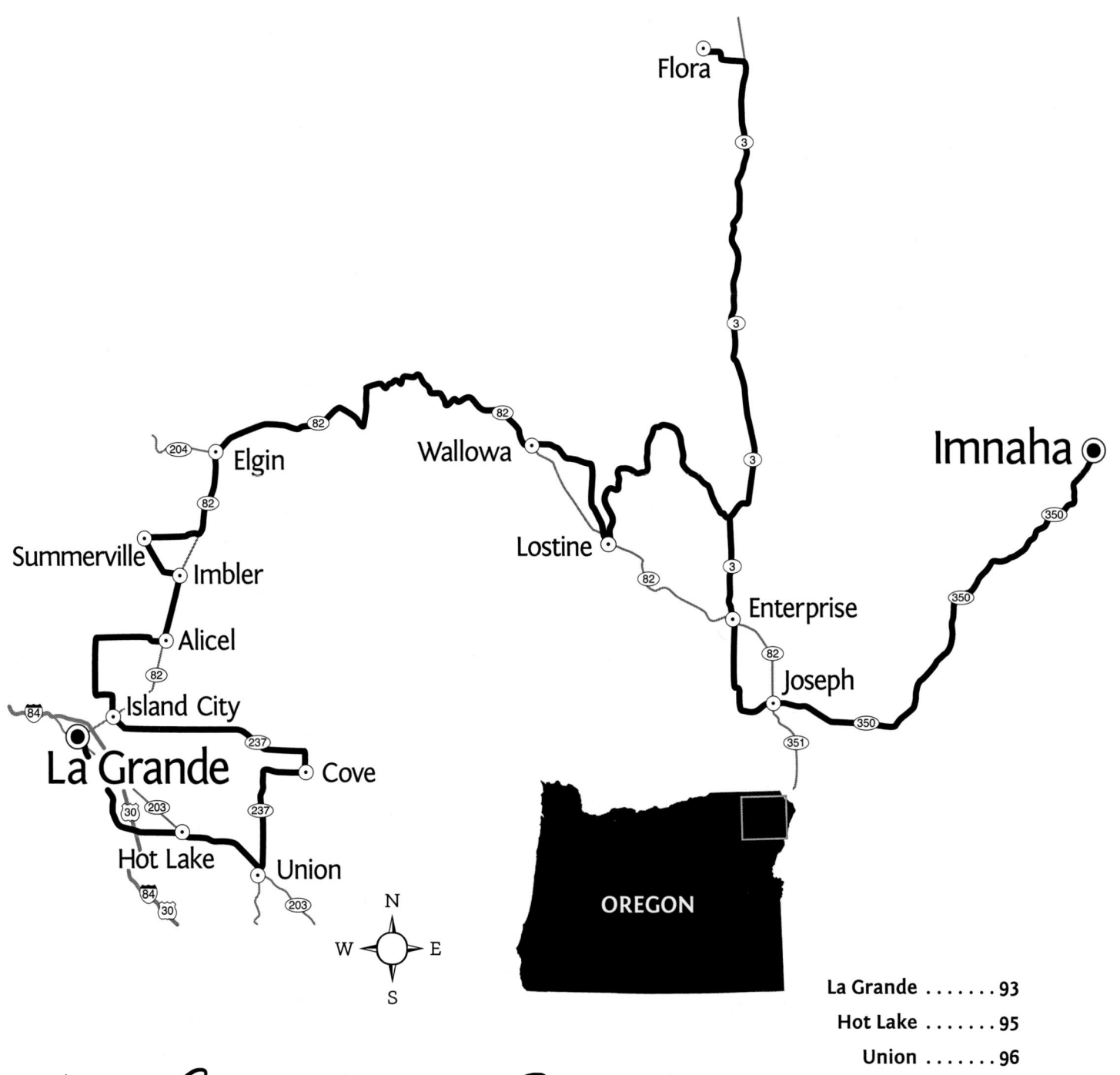

La Grande to Imnaha

La Grande	93
Hot Lake	95
Union	96
Cove	98
Island City	99
Alicel	101
Imbler	102
Summerville	103
Elgin	104
Wallowa	106
Lostine	109
Flora	112
Enterprise	113
Joseph	115
Imnaha	118

From the Grande Ronde Valley to the Wallowa Mountains
La Grande to Imnaha (141 miles)

Follow the Oregon Trail from the banks of the Grande Ronde River at La Grande to Hot Lake, the largest hot spring in the United States and site of an 1812 trading post. From there, journey to Union, settled by northern sympathizers during the Civil War.

More naturally heated mineral springs occur at Cove, the next stop en route to Island City, which was, at one time, completely surrounded by water. From Island City, venture to Alicel, a community with as many grain elevators as homes.

The route continues to Imbler, Grass Seed Capital of the World, where sausage is sold by the foot. In Elgin, visit the museum or take in a movie at the near century old Opera House. Learn about the Nez Perce at Wallowa and visit the tribe's traditional home at Lostine.

From Lostine, drive nearly fifty scenic miles that follow the Nez Perce migration route, turning north-bound into the Wallowa Whitman National Forest, past the Joseph Canyon overlook to the ghost town, Flora. Return to the 120 year old cities of Enterprise and Joseph, only eight miles apart.

the Wallowa Mountains

Spectacular peaks of the Wallowa Mountains, home of Chief Joseph, rise near the town that bears the chief's name. Scores of recreational opportunities in the Wallowa Mountains and Eagle Cap Wilderness Area are accessed through the gateway communities of Wallowa, Lostine, Enterprise and Joseph. Conclude the trip in Imnaha, home of the annual "Rattlesnake and Bear Feed."

La Grande

Elevation: 2784 feet

Location:
45.32.718 N • 118.09.323 W

Services: gas, food, lodging, RV, B&B

Homesteading pioneers founded the community of La Grande on the banks of the Grande Ronde River, Oregon's second longest free flowing river (only the John Day is longer). Benjamin Brown, the first settler in the area, chose the site for the new community. Called Brown Town in 1861 and Brownsville in 1862, the name changed to La Grande in 1863. La Grande, now the Union County seat of government, incorporated in 1864, the same year the county was officially formed. When the railroad came to La Grande in 1884, a new town was created because the tracks missed the old town by a mile. Fires in 1874, 1886 and 1891 devastated the downtown business area. The Oregon Trail came through what is now "B Avenue."

Frank Lloyd Wright designed prairie-style house

Points of Interest

- **City Hall** *(1000 Adams)*
  Built in the 1890s.

- **Rail Station** *(On Jefferson between Depot and Chestnut)*
  This is the old depot.

- **Charles Conkey House** *(806 Main)*
  In 1892, this home cost $1800 to build.

- **Queen Anne-Style house** *(702 Spring)*
  1907 beauty with 'fish scale' siding and leaded glass windows.

- **Methodist Church** *(905 Spring)*
  1872.

- **Stange Manor** *(1612 Walnut)*
  Originally built on two acres, this 1924 home is over 7800 square feet.

- **La Grande Visitors Center and Eastern Oregon Fire Museum** *(102 Elm)*
  This old firehouse was used from 1899 to 2002.

- **Old Houses**
  (1602, 1704, 1708 and 1710 2nd)
  1906 Classic Revival home of Walter Brenholts, 1907 Bohenkamp house (known as the "castle"), Craftsman-Style ordered from Sears-Roebuck, and 1895 Eastlake-Style, respectively.

- **Episcopal Church** *(4th and O)*
  Built in 1924 of volcanic tuft and designed by the Miller house architect.

- **Prairie-Style House** *(709 O)*
  Built in 1900, it was designed by Frank Lloyd Wright.

- **Charles Miller House** *(1502 4th)*
  1924 English Tudor design with leaded glass windows.

- **John Anthony House** *(1696 6th)*
  1890 Eastlake-style.

- **Eastern Oregon University** *(8th and K)*
  Founded in 1929.

- **Calvary Cemetery and Hillcrest Cemeteries** *(12th and G)*
  The two cemeteries, dating to the 1870s, are across the street from each other.

- **Birnie Park** *(B and Gekeler)*
  Formerly an emigrant camping and assembly area. A full-sized covered wagon replica is displayed here.

- **Gangloff Park** *(Pioneer Drive)*
  Gangloff was a pioneer and nurseryman. An old log cabin, moved to this location, is a featured attraction.

old fire engine at Eastern Oregon Fire Museum

Bohenkamp House ("the castle")

La Grande to Hot Lake

Distance:
9.8 miles

Directions:
From the intersection of Adams and Spruce, turn left, heading east.

Points En Route

(mileage from the intersection of Adams Avenue and Spruce Street)

0.6 miles:
At the corner of Highway 30 and 20th Street, turn right onto 20th Street toward the Department of Fish and Wildlife Building.

0.7 miles:
The Department of Fish and Wildlife and State Forestry Building.

0.8 miles:
La Grande Drive-In Theater.

1.1 miles:
Cross Gekeler Lane and keep left on Foothill Road, following the Oregon Scenic Tour Route. The Grandview Cemetery, which dates to the 1880s, is to the right.

1.2 miles:
Red, square barn.

1.7 miles:
Series of old outbuildings.

2.3 miles:
Picturesque barns.

2.7 miles:
Old farmhouse.

3.5 miles:
Another old farmhouse.

4.8 miles:
Ladd Marsh Wildlife Refuge.

6.6 miles:
Junction of I-84. Continue over the freeway.

6.8 miles:
Nature Trailhead into the refuge.

6.9 miles:
Go right on Pierce Road. Pavement ends (2.9 miles of good gravel).

7.0 miles:
Turn left onto Hot Lake Lane.

9.2 miles:
Eagles Hot Lake RV Park.

9.7 miles:
Intersection of Hot Lake Lane and Highway 203. Turn right on Highway 203.

9.8 miles:
Hot Lake

Hot Lake

Elevation: 2690 feet

Location:
45.14.600 N • 117.57.511 W

Services: food, lodging

Hot Lake Spring is the largest of its kind in the world. Every day, 2.5 million gallons of 208-degree water, from over 10,000 feet below the ground surface, are released. The lake lies over a fault that extends along the base of a mountain. In 1812, Robert Stuart visited Hot Lake on his way to Astoria, the same year a trading post was established at this location. The trading post is a cave-like structure dug near the base of a hill. Pioneers reportedly could smell, from a great distance, the sulfur fumes emitting from the water and stopped at the lake as they progressed toward the Willamette Valley.

Hot Lake Hotel

The first wooden structure near the lake was erected in 1864. The railroad came to Hot Lake in 1883, the same year the post office opened. In 1905, a 65,000 square foot, brick, 105-room resort hotel was constructed. Additional rooms built of wood were added later. The elevator, located in the brick portion of the hotel, is the second oldest on the west coast. In 1917, the third floor of the resort became a hospital and was referred to as the "Mayo Clinic of the West." Written on a third floor wall, in 1918, is the reminder to "Keep your voice low and be sweet."

Between 1920 and 1934, the resort and clinic reached their peak in popularity, until a 1934 fire destroyed over 200 of the rooms. In 1939, World War II pilot and nursing schools were established here. The hotel became a nursing home in the 1950s and later the resort operated as a series of enterprises, including a nightclub, fish hatchery, restaurants, bathhouses, and condos. In 2005, artist David Manuel and his family purchased the property and began resort renovation and restoration. Plans include a fire truck and stagecoach museum, B&B, restaurant, spa, servicemen's memorial, bronze foundry and art gallery. Several of David Manuel's impressive bronze sculptures adorn the grounds. The artist can be found sculpting or painting in private family quarters here.

Points of Interest

- **Hot Lake Hotel**
  Constructed from 1906-1909 to replace the original 1864 building.

- **Hot Lake Springs**
  The hot water is cooled for therapy baths.

- **1812 Trading Post**
  Located on the Oregon Trail and on resort property. Open to visitors.

- **Art Gallery**
  David Manuel bronzes and paintings are displayed and available for purchase.

1812 Trading Post

Hot Springs to Union

Distance:
4.6 miles

Directions:
From the entrance to the resort, turn right onto Highway 30, heading east toward Union.

Points En Route

(mileage from the entrance to the resort)

Numerous old farms and barns stand along Highway 30 en route to Union.

4.6 miles:
Union

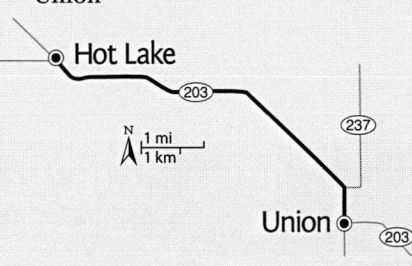

Little White Church

Union

Elevation: 2810 feet

Location:
45.12.454 N • 117.51.927 W

Services: gas, food, lodging, B&B

With a population of 2,215 people, Union is the second largest city in Union County. Once the county seat, it was a bitter rival with La Grande for governmental control. In 1862, E.H. Lewis, Samuel Hannah and Fred Nodine, who favored the north during the Civil War, founded Union.

Historic Union Hotel

Conrad Miller settled here in 1862, planted apple and pear trees, and began the first nursery in the Grande Ronde Valley. The Union post office opened in 1863. Carved from Baker County in 1864, Union County is over 2000 square miles in area. By 1865, Union had a livery stable, Wells Fargo stage stop, flourmill and mercantile store. Union was an important transportation hub that provided mining supplies to the Cornucopia Mining District. It had its own college in 1890. Today it is a key agricultural center and Main Street is designated a National Historic District.

Points of Interest

- **Wilson Dry Goods Store** *(101 Main)*
  Built in 1890. The local bordello was located upstairs.

- **Union Drug Store** *(105 Main)*
  Operating as a drug store since 1903. Dentists once occupied the second floor.

- **Union Bank Building** *(181 Main)*
  Old photos hang on the walls of the 1910 building.

- **Union Library** *(182 Main)*
  Carnegie funds helped to build this library in 1902. It is the second smallest Carnegie Library in the United States.

- **Woodward Saloon** *(206 Main)*
  Built in 1900 and now houses a liquor store and hardware store.

- **Union Confectionary Store** *(267 Main)*
  Built in 1898.

Union

Points of Interest (continued)

- **Masonic Temple** (*268 Main*)
  In 1898, the downstairs was the Townley-Gale mercantile store and the upstairs the Masonic lodge. Today the lower floor of the building is the post office.

- **Levy Building** (*306 Main*)
  The 1870 mercantile sold grain, wool, hides and food. This is the first brick building in Union.

- **Historic Union Hotel** (*326 Main*)
  Built in 1921 and restored in the 1990s.

- **Union City Hall** (*342 Main*)
  Built in 1891.

- **Little White Church** (*366 Main*)
  Early Methodist settlers built this church in 1873.

- **Eaton House** (*464 Main*)
  Eaton was a business owner who profited from freighting, ranching and farming. The house contains two large bank vaults.

- **Thomson House** (*475 Main*)
  1873 Victorian-style. Thomson owned the planing mill that operated on Main Street.

- **Union High School** (*540 Main*)
  Built on the site of the old Union County Courthouse. The boiler room is located in what was the county jail.

- **Union County Museum** (*Main and Dearborn*)
  "Cowboys, Now and Then" is a featured exhibit.

- **Union Mercantile** (*Main and Arch*)
  Opened in 1898.

- **Wright House** (*429 Bellwood*)
  William Wright, president of the bank, built this house in 1882. His daughter married Dr. Phy, the builder of Hot Lakes Sanatorium.

- **Wildwood Home** (*101 E Bryan*)
  The oldest home in Union, built in 1869 by Mendal Israel.

- **Queen Anne-Style House** (*369 Bryan*)
  Built in the 1870s.

- **Townley House** (*782 5th*)
  The mercantile storeowner built this house in 1892.

- **Union Victorian Cemetery** (*770 E. Fulton*)
  Dates to 1862.

- **Oregon State Agriculture Experimental Station** (*Arch and 10th*)
  Built in 1901. One of the oldest OSU Agricultural Stations.

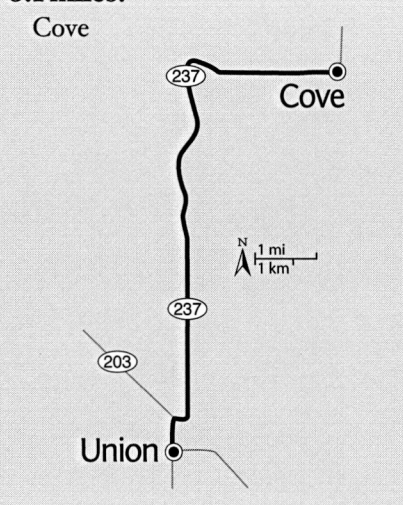

Eaton House

Union to Cove

Distance:
8.1 miles

Directions:
From the intersection of Main and Bryan, go east on Bryan.

Points En Route

(mileage the intersection of Main and Bryan)

0.2 miles:
Keep left. Bryan Street becomes Highway 237 (Cove Highway).

0.3 miles:
Grand, Victorian houses on both sides of the highway.

2.2 miles:
Small, abandoned house with two front doors.

5.8 miles:
Expansive views of pastureland and view of Cove.

7.8 miles:
Victorian house.

8.1 miles:
Cove

Cove

Elevation: 2960 feet

Location:
45.17.809 N • 117.48.671

Services: gas, food, RV, camping

Originally known as "Forest Cove," the community is nestled below 7,132-foot Mt. Fanny. Mt. Fanny was named to honor Fanny Cowles, who settled here in 1862 and was the first white woman to climb the mountain. The name Forest Cove was shortened to Cove in 1868, amid clamor by early residents. The first store and gristmill opened in 1866 and the first sawmill in 1869. Fires in 1919 and 1921 destroyed most of the old businesses and homes.

old barn

Points of Interest

- **Forest Cove Warm Springs Pool** (*860 Water*)
  A retreat center, complete with a pool, sauna, RV and camping facilities. Natural hot spring water fills the municipal pool.

- **Episcopal Church**
  (*Ascension and School*)
  The 1876 church is the oldest in Cove. The private school opened in 1884.

- **Calvary Baptist Church**
  (*Main and French*)
  Circa 1900.

- **City Library** (*600 Main*)
  The 1900 library was moved to this location in 1924. On display is early Cove memorabilia.

- **Old Jail**
  (*next to the post office at 603 Main*)
  Built to withstand fire.

- **Cement Block Store** (*604 Main*)
  Built in the 1920s, also to resist fire.

- **Old School** (*803 Main*)
  1915.

- **Old House** (*Mill*)
  Constructed in 1906.

- **Old House**
  (*1007 Orchard*)
  A grand home in its day.

- **Gilstrap Winery**
  (*69789 Antles Lane*)
  The only winery in Eastern Oregon.

- **Cove Cemetery**
  (*68714 2nd*)
  Located south of town on the hill. Dating to the 1880s.

- **Old Barn**
  (*1307 Jasper*)
  Survived the fires.

Episcopal Church

Cove to Island City

Distance:
12.8 miles

Directions:
From the intersection of Main and French, take Main north as it curves to follow Highway 237.

Points En Route

(mileage from Main and French)

0.6 miles:
At corner of Highway 30 and 20th Street, turn right onto 20th Street toward the Department of Fish and Wildlife Building.

0.5 miles:
Historic barn, constructed in 1860.

0.9 miles:
Artisian Water Bottling Company.

1.1 miles:
Cove Grange Hall. Keep left on Highway 237, heading toward Island City.

1.6 miles:
The old Shanghai School.

2.1 miles:
Century Farm.

10.2 miles:
House with two front doors.

12.8 miles:
Island City

Grain Elevator

Island City

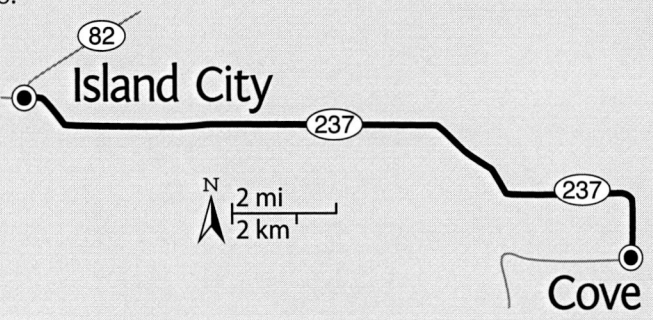

Elevation: 2774 feet

Location:
45.20.428 N • 118.02.866 W

Services: gas, food, lodging

Island City was formed in 1872, with roots as a business center for wheat and flour production. The community was originally platted on an eight by one and a half-mile island surrounded by the Grande Ronde River. The water was later diverted and island status lost. President US Grant signed the 1872 papers of incorporation and the town was chartered in 1904.

Points of Interest

- **Grain Elevator** *(10103 D)*
  The old elevator and feed store now house Island City Glass.

- **Fred Beeman Community Park** *(5th and McAlister)*
  Restrooms, playfield, picnic.

- **Island City Fire Department** *(10200 McCalister)*
  Old and vacant.

- **Two-story House** *(10301 McAlister)*
  Old with noteworthy stained glass windows.

- **Island City Cemetery** *(McAlister)*
  The 1870s cemetery is uniquely set next to a golf and country club.

Island City to Alicel

Distance:
10.6 miles

Directions:
At the intersection of Highway 82 and McAlister, go north on McAlister.

Points En Route

(mileage from the intersection of Highway 82 and McAlister)

0.2 miles:
At the intersection of McAlister Road and Hunter Road, go left on Hunter.

0.8 miles:
Old farmhouse.

1.2 miles:
Aging farm and outbuildings.

1.4 miles:
At the yellow flashing light, turn left onto Booth Lane.

2.0 miles:
Colorful, old farm and barns.

2.5 miles:
Turn right onto Mt. Glen Road.

3.3 miles:
Cemetery, dating to the 1870s.

4.2 miles:
Pioneer Monument. The marker, difficult to locate near the house at 63822 on the left side of the highway, reads, "In 1861, Ben and Frances Brown stayed the winter at this location." Brown was founder of La Grande.

4.7 miles:
Old schoolhouse.

5.7 miles:
Turn right onto Standley Lane.

7.0 miles:
At the intersection of Mt. Glen and Standley Lane, stay on Standley.

7.5 miles:
Pavement ends.

8.0 miles:
Pavement returns.

8.1 miles:
Farmhouse with unusual cupola and stained glass windows.

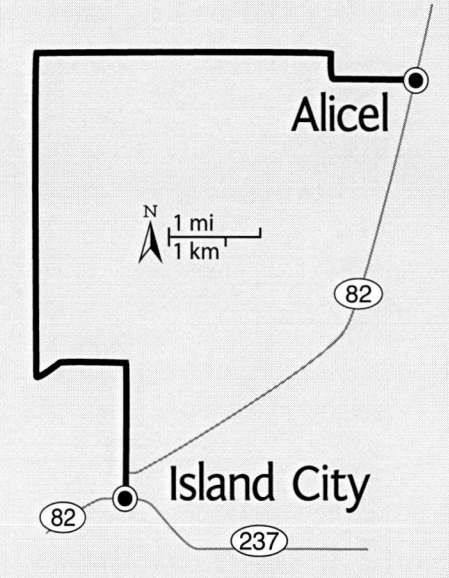

8.5 miles:
At the intersection with Webster Road, continue straight ahead on Standley. Pavement ends.

9.7 miles:
Intersection with Sandridge. Stay on Standley.

10.3 miles:
Pavement returns.

10.4 miles:
Intersection with Highway 82. Cross the highway. Standley becomes Alicel Lane.

10.6 miles:
(Depot Drive) Alicel

former schoolhouse along road to Alicel

Alicel

Elevation: 2778 feet

Location:
45.24.327 N • 117.58.469 W

Services: none

Alicel is located in the heart of the Grande Ronde Valley, where numerous grain elevators dot the landscape. Charles Ladd built the railroad branch line in 1890 and named the station after his wife, Alice L. Ladd. Alicel is a small, unincorporated community. The Alicel post office opened in 1890 and closed in 1972.

Old House

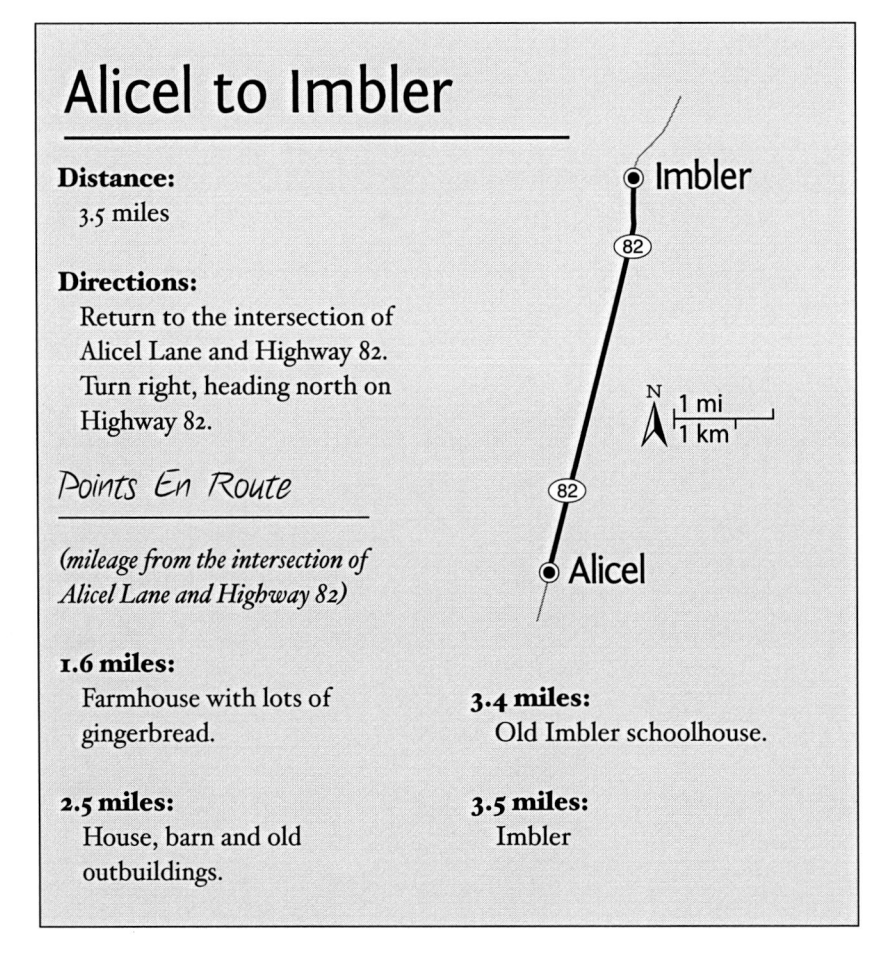

Points of Interest

- **Old Houses**
  Several older houses line Depot Drive.

- **Alicel School** *(Seventh Drive)*
  The 1919 school is now a private residence.

- **Grain Elevators**
  Located near the railroad tracks.

Alicel to Imbler

Distance:
3.5 miles

Directions:
Return to the intersection of Alicel Lane and Highway 82. Turn right, heading north on Highway 82.

Points En Route

(mileage from the intersection of Alicel Lane and Highway 82)

1.6 miles:
Farmhouse with lots of gingerbread.

2.5 miles:
House, barn and old outbuildings.

3.4 miles:
Old Imbler schoolhouse.

3.5 miles:
Imbler

Imbler

Elevation: 2732 feet

Location:
45.27.419 N • 117.57.756 W

Services: gas, food

The first settler in the area, Joseph Harris, arrived in 1865. Harris Mountain is named after him. Imbler was platted in 1891 by settler Jesse Imbler, for whom the town was named. The post office opened in 1891 and Jesse's brother, Albert, was appointed the first postmaster. Known as the "Grass Seed Capital of the World," Imbler incorporated in 1922 and is home to 380 people. Imbler is an important grain shipping point. A flourmill stood on the property where the present school is built. At one time, orchards dotted the area and fruit packing sheds lined the railroad tracks. Imbler has many Century Farms.

Points of Interest

- **Imbler Market**
  (Main and Ruckman)
  The store, built in 1904, sells pepperoni sausage by the foot.

- **Imbler Methodist Community Church**
  (Hull and Ruckman)
  Early 1900s.

- **Union City Cooperative Association Building**
  (Main and Ruckman)
  Vacant and over 100 years old.

- **Imbler Schools** *(6th and 7th)*
  Built in 1916. The building on the grounds in front of the school was constructed in the 1870s and is the oldest in town. It is used as the school district music room.

- **Old Houses**
  (520, 610 and 680 Ruckman)
  All over 100 years old.

- **Imbler Christian Church**
  (5th and Ruckman)
  Still in use.

Imbler Country Market

Imbler to Summerville

Distance:
2.9 miles

Directions:
From the intersection of Main and Ruckman, go north on Ruckman (Highway 82).

Points En Route

(mileage from the Imbler Store)

0.2 miles:
At the "Y" in the road, veer left on Brooks Road and go left onto Summerville Road.

1.2 miles:
Steeter Farms.

1.9 miles:
Summerville Cemetery. Dates to the early 1900s.

1.9 miles:
Old farmhouse on Sandridge Lane.

2.9 miles:
Summerville

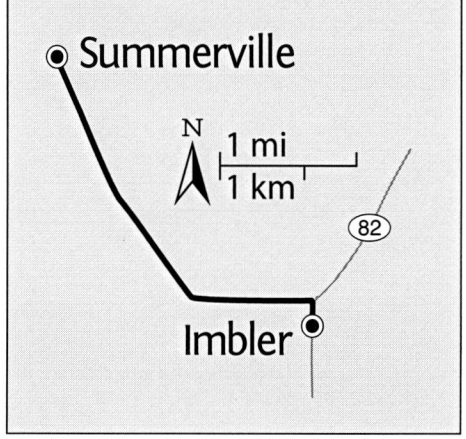

Summerville

Elevation: 2705 feet

Location:
45.29.393 N • 118.00.162 W

Services: none

Summerville was an important stage stop on the George Thomas Line in 1865. The stage line ceased operation in 1868 with a brief return in 1873. Summerville was named to honor Alexander Summerville, a friend of the first postmaster. The town incorporated in 1885. At its peak in 1889, Summerville had a bank, hotel, brewery, drugstore, butcher shop, two flourmills, two blacksmiths, several saloons, three churches, three dress stores, four merchandise stores, and four sawmills. It rapidly declined when the railroad was routed through Elgin rather than here.

Points of Interest

- **Old Store** (301 Main)
  Also a post office and tavern.

- **IOOF Hall** (309 Main)
  Built in 1874 and is the tallest building in town.

- **Community Hall**
  (Donvegen and Patten)
  A small park is adjacent.

storefront in Summerville

Summerville to Elgin

Distance:
8.4 miles

Directions:
Continue northwest on Main Street (Summerville Road).

Points En Route

(mileage from the store)

0.1 miles:
Turn right onto Courtney Lane. There is a historical marker indicating the site of the 1870 Summerville Stockade, which was built by early settlers for protection against Indian uprisings.

0.3 miles:
Abandoned homestead.

1.0 miles:
Old, whitewashed farm.

1.8 and 2.2 miles:
Huge nests on poles.

2.9 miles:
Creek and man-made pond.

3.7 miles:
At the intersection of Courtney Lane and Highway 82, go left on Highway 82 toward Elgin.

4.0 miles:
Rinehart Lane. Site of Rinehart.

5.1 miles:
Crossing the Grande Ronde River and views of the ravine.

8.1 miles:
Crossing the river.

8.4 miles:
Elgin

Elgin

Elevation: 2670 feet

Location:
45.03.353 N • 117.54.985 W

Services: gas, food, lodging

Elgin is located at the base of the Wallowa Mountains on the Grande Ronde River and was an important gathering place for the Nez Perce Indians. By 1882, Elgin was an important trade center. The post office opened in 1885 and the community incorporated in 1891 after the Oregon Railway branch line came through the area in 1890. The name Elgin was inspired by a song that was popular at the time, entitled "Lost on the Lady Elgin." Fires in 1920 and 1930 took their toll on the downtown businesses. The Hill Spring Fountain, now located in Witty Park on 8th Avenue, was relocated to this spot from its original location on old Highway 82 (near the river canyon south of town). It provided travelers with fresh water for many years. Every July, Elgin hosts the Elgin Stampede PRCA Rodeo.

Elgin City Hall

Points of Interest

- **Elgin Opera House** *(104 8th)*
  Built in 1912 as the City Hall and Elgin Opera House. Movies are still shown and a museum is located here.

- **Elgin City Jail** *(104 8th)*
  Constructed in 1897 and located behind the Opera House.

- **Hindman House**
  (Baltimore and 6th)
  This elaborately decorated home was built in 1897.

- **Methodist Church**
  (7th and Birch)
  Originally built as a Baptist Church in 1888. Methodists bought the building in 1930 shortly after fire destroyed their 1907 church building.

- **Sommer Hotel** *(45-47 8th)*
  Built of brick in 1903, next to a wooden structure that burned in the 1920 fire.

- **Myers Meat Market** *(93 8th)*
  Early 1900s construction.

- **Hardware store and IOOF Building** *(8th and Division)*
  Built as a drug store in 1897. IOOF took over the building in 1903.

- **First Bank of Elgin**
  (8th and Alder)
  Built in 1898.

- **Masterson House** *(307 8th)*
  The house, made from local bricks, was constructed on one square block and had a barn, pasture, orchard, icehouse and garden.

- **Ford Garage** *(831 Alder)*
  1912 garage and dealership.

Elgin City Jail

Elgin

Points of Interest (continued)

- **Elgin Fire Department** (*900 Alder*)
  Built with locally made brick in 1918.

- **Allen House** (*900 Division*)
  1895 with additions in 1911 and 1940.

- **NAPA Auto Parts** (*997 Division*)
  An 1887 Fruit Warehouse.

- **Hotchkiss House** (*55 10th*)
  The 1895 home of Dr. Kirby and the first residence built with local brick.

- **Elgin Hospital** (*1000 Division*)
  Built as a private residence and later used as the hospital in 1915.

- **Mays House** (*1001 Division*)
  Warehouse owner and Elgin's second mayor, Robert Mays, elected in 1894, built his house in 1891.

- **Highland Cemetery** (*4 miles east of town on Good Road*)
  Dates to 1881.

Mays House

Elgin to Wallowa

Distance:
24.7 miles

Directions:
From the intersection of Albany and North 6th, drive northeast on the Wallowa Lake Highway (Highway 82).

Points En Route

(mileage from Albany and N 6th)

0.1 miles:
Crossing the Grande Ronde River.

2.8 miles:
Old barns.

4.9 miles:
Old farm with outbuildings.

12.6 miles:
Entering Wallowa County.

13.0 miles:
The Minam post office opened in 1890, closed in 1891 and was reestablished in 1910 when the railroad came through. Minam is located at the confluence of the Wallowa and the Minam Rivers.

13.1 miles:
Access road to Minam State Park. Twelve primitive campsites among large pines, river fishing and rafting.

15.6 miles:
Wallowa River Wayside. Picnic, restrooms, fishing.

18.6 miles:
Fountain Wayside. Picnic and restrooms.

20.8 miles:
Crossing Rock Creek.

23.5 miles:
Picturesque barn.

23.9 miles:
Old house and barn.

24.4 miles:
Crossing the Wallowa River.

24.7 miles:
Wallowa

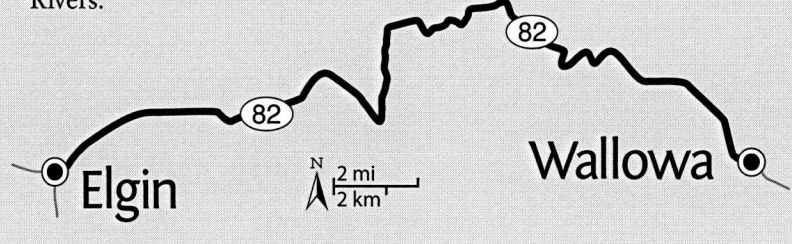

Wallowa

Elevation: 2923 feet

Location:
45.34.354 N • 117.31.621 W

Services: gas, food, lodging, B&B, RV

Wallowa lies in the broad valley north of the beautiful Wallowa Mountains that are called the "Switzerland of America." Locals believe that this is paradise, and are willing to share it with visitors drawn to the natural beauty of the area. Six families that hoped to farm in the Grande Ronde River Basin's fertile ground, settled here in 1872. The first post office opened in 1873, the town was platted in 1889, and incorporated in 1899. Passenger trains steamed into Wallowa in 1908 on track laid from Elgin and the community grew quickly after that. Wallowa is a Nez Perce word (Wa-La-Wah) that describes a set of stakes used to trap fish. Area economy is fueled by the typical eastern Oregon triad of farming, ranching and timber and rounded out by tourism and other entrepreneurial ventures. Wallowa is a gateway to many of the hiking trails of the spectacular Eagle Cap Wilderness. Other recreational activities include camping, fishing, snow sports, and more.

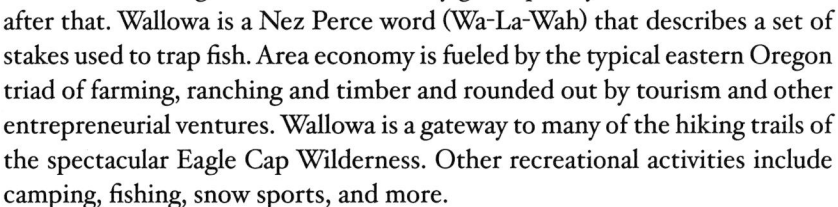

Former United Methodist Church

Points of Interest

- **United Methodist Church** *(202 1st)*
  Built in 1899.

- **Stockgrowers and Farmers National Bank** *(218 1st)*
  1905.

- **Wallowa Theater** *(307 1st)*
  Built in 1919, and now an antique store. The stage and projection room are identifiable.

- **Holmes House** *(308 1st)*
  Built between 1892 and 1895 by E.A. Holmes. A doctor lived here in the 1940s and added an office (east of the residence).

- **Emory Rognas House** *(701 1st)*
  A 1910 Craftsman bungalow.

- **Drug Store** *(1st)*
  Operated from 1897 to 2008.

- **Telephone Office** *(1st and Storie)*
  Opened in 1917.

- **Wallowa Band Nez Perce Trail Interpretive Center** *(2nd and Storie)*
  Adjacent to City Hall in the old bank building.

- **Knights of Columbus** *(Storie)*
  Built in the 1920s.

- **Haisten House** *(302 Storie)*
  Queen Anne-Style, built between 1895 and 1905.

- **Colonial Revival Style House** *(308 Storie)*
  Built about 1911.

- **McClaran House** *(406 Storie)*
  Craftsman-Style, built in 1909.

- **Wallowa Library** *(1st and Pine)*
  Originally the meat market.

McClaran House

Wallowa

Points of Interest (continued)

- **General Mercantile Store** *(1st and Pine)*
  Opened as a mercantile and post office in 1906.

- **Wallowa Hardware** *(1st and Pine)*
  1896. Originally the Eastern Oregon Mercantile Company.

- **Morelock Building** *(1st and Spruce)*
  In 1916, a car dealership replaced the livery stable at this location.

- **Wallowa High School** *(1st and Douglas)*
  Opened in 1922, replacing the 1899 wooden structure.

- **Hetrich House** *(101 2nd)*
  1898 Eastlake-Style cottage.

- **Church of Christ** *(102 Alder)*
  Built in 1907 as the Presbyterian Church.

- **Holmes House** *(101 Holmes)*
  1910 Craftsman, built for the son of E.A. Holmes.

- **Thomas DeVault House** *(104 Holmes)*
  Built in 1903. The foundation is Bowlby Stone, material that is soft when unearthed and quickly hardens.

- **Couch House** *(303 Holmes)*
  1910 Colonial Revival.

- **Spence Family House** *(402 Holmes)*
  Built in 1912.

- **IOOF Lodge #154** *(0.3 miles southeast of downtown on Highway 82)*
  Dates to the early 1900s.

barn in Wallowa

Stockgrowers and Farmers National Bank

Wallowa to Lostine

Distance:
8.7 miles

Directions:
From 1st Street (Highway 82) and Whiskey Creek Road, drive east on Whiskey Creek Road.

Points En Route

(mileage from the corner of 1st and Whiskey Creek Road)

0.0 miles:
Just past the intersection is the site of the Wallowa Flour Mill. The canal was constructed to divert water to the mill.

0.1 miles:
RV Park.

0.2 miles:
Riverside Drive, a street of older homes.

0.3 miles:
TamKaLiks, sacred ground to the Nez Perce and setting for an annual Friendship Feast and Pow Wow.

1.1 miles:
Wallowa Cemetery, dates to the 1890s.

1.6 miles:
Turn right onto Jim Town Road. (Jim Town is also spelled Jimtown)

2.5 miles:
Junction with Baker Road. Stay on Jim Town.

3.2 miles:
Gravel.

4.2 miles:
Intersection with Warnock. Turn right onto Warnock Road.

4.5 miles:
Crossing railroad tracks.

4.7 miles:
The Wallowa River.

6.2 miles:
Lostine Canyon. Views of the Wallowa Mountains.

7.8 miles:
Road to Lostine Cemetery, 1880s.

8.7 miles:
Lostine

abandoned house outside Lostine

Lostine

Elevation: 3271 feet

Location:
45.29.227 N • 117.25.911 W

Services: food

Lostine is a scenic farming town that was the traditional home of the Nez Perce. Chief Joseph died in 1871 and was buried here until his remains were moved to the foot of Wallowa Lake in 1927. In 1878, W.R. Laughlin built a small cabin and settled in what is now known as Lostine. In that same year, a post office was established and Laughlin was appointed postmaster. He named the town after his former residence in Lostine, Kansas. As the community grew, many businesses opened and thrived, largely due to the Joseph and Elgin Stage Line that passed through. A terrible fire in 1893 leveled most of the businesses and homes. Lostine rebuilt and incorporated in 1903. Lostine is platted next to a river of the same name. The Eagle Cap Wilderness can be accessed from the road that follows the Lostine River through a scenic canyon. Lostine hosts a huge 4th of July Flea Market, the community's longest standing tradition.

Lostine School

Points of Interest:

- **Magill House** *(113 State)*
  Built about 1898.

- **Crow House** *(115 State)*
  The Lostine Flour Mill, which burned in 1893, stood next to this 1905 house.

- **Lostine Meat Market**
  (on State next to the antique store)
  Opened in 1890.

- **Martin House** *(118 State)*
  Built about 1916 from lumber salvaged from the old livery stable.

- **Foster House** *(119 State)*
  Frank Foster, a retired farmer, had this home built about 1895.

- **Noland Hotel** *(123 State)*
  Built about 1905. Located next to the Lostine Tavern.

- **McKenzie Drug Store**
  (125 State)
  Built in the late 1890s and now the Lostine Tavern.

- **City Hall** *(128 State)*
  Also houses the library and an upstairs jail.

- **Lostine City Park**
  (Behind the City Hall)
  Playground and picnic area.

- **Fleenor House** *(141 State)*
  The Fleenors ran the livery stable and the buggy and wagon rental business from their 1895 house.

Fleenor House

- **Lostine Grange #605**
  (State Street)
  Built in the 1920s.

- **Lostine Presbyterian Church**
  (State and Resort)
  The church was organized in 1885 and the building was constructed in 1888.

- **Lostine Bank** *(State and Wallowa)*
  Built in 1890.

- **Commercial Building**
  (State and Wallowa)
  The building looks much as it did when built in 1905. The IOOF and the Rebekahs hold lodge meetings on the second floor.

- **Crow and Company Building**
  (State and Wallowa)
  Owned by Crow family since 1906. Originally housed the Lostine Mercantile. A doctor and a dentist practiced in the second story.

- **Lostine School**
  (Wallowa and College)
  Built of Bowlby Stone in 1902 and now a private school and community center.

- **McCubbin House** *(409 Wallowa)*
  This 1906 Gothic-style house belonged to John and Maryette McCubbin, who came to Lostine in 1877.

- **Poley House** *(905 Forest)*
  Built in 1890.

- **Goodman House** *(909 Forest)*
  The Goodmans were sheep ranchers who built this Colonial Revival home in 1905.

Goodman House

Lostine Tavern

Lostine Hotel

Lostine to Flora

Distance:
49.6 miles

Directions:
From the intersection of Wallowa Street and State (Highway 82), go east on Wallowa Street.

Points En Route

(mileage from the intersection of Wallowa and State)

0.1 miles:
Turn left onto Jim Town Road.

1.3 miles:
Site of Evans (corner of Clark and Jim Town). This small community was formed in 1909 when the railroad missed Lostine. A rail station was built here and Evans became the center for trade. Evans had its own post office from 1913 to 1940. At one time Evans had a church, school, train depot, two stores, three wheat warehouses and a dozen homes.

1.5 miles:
Railroad tracks and gravel road (next 13.3 miles).

3.5 miles:
Crossing the Wallowa River.

3.5 miles:
Intersection with Leap Lane. Go straight on Leap Lane.

3.6 miles:
Unique, interesting concrete structure with an arch opening.

3.7 miles:
Parsnip Creek on the right.

3.8 miles:
Old farmhouse and outbuildings.

7.4 miles:
Old car and buildings. Go left, staying on Leap Lane.

9.8 miles:
Weather vane, old farm and outbuildings.

9.9 miles:
Lathrop Family Century Farm.

12.3 miles:
Stay right.

12.6 miles:
Excellent view of the Wallowa Mountains.

14.8 miles:
Pavement returns.

19.0 miles:
Old granary and farm.

19.1 miles:
Intersection of Leap Lane and Highway 3. Go left on Highway 3.

19.5 miles:
The highway follows Trout Creek and the Nez Perce migration route.

22.2 miles:
Trout Creek Ranch.

26.4 miles:
Entering Open Range land.

30.6 miles:
Entering the Wallowa-Whitman National Forest.

33.0 miles:
Summit, 4693 feet.

34.1 miles:
Sled Springs Work Center.

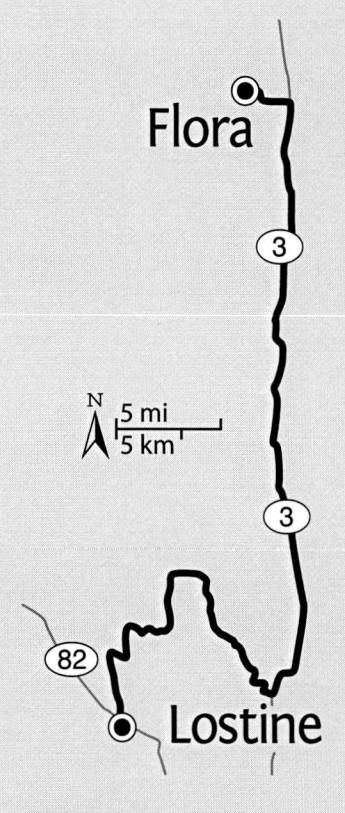

35.0 miles:
Site of Sled Springs, a former stage stop.

39.0 miles:
Leaving the Wallowa-Whitman National Forest.

42.8 miles:
Flora Highway Maintenance Station.

43.0 miles:
Look down on Joseph Creek, officially declared a Wild River. This is the birth place of Chief Joseph. Below the view point (to the right) is a cave where the Nez Perce stored supplies and provisions.

47.0 miles:
Turn left on Flora Lane, heading toward Flora.

49.6 miles:
Flora

Flora

Elevation: 4633 feet

Location:
45.54.067 N • 117.18.580 W

Services: none

The Flora post office, named for the daughter of postmaster A.D. Bussard, opened in 1890 and closed in 1966. The community was platted in 1897 but never incorporated. In 1900, Flora had a bank, school, newspaper, livery stable, post office, Methodist Church and parsonage, Catholic Church, the Farmer's Hotel, and two stores. Several families live year-round in Flora.

Points of Interest

- **Flora School** *(College)*
  Built in 1915 and undergoing restoration.

- **Flora Church**
  Next to the school, built in the early 1900s.

- **Livery Stable**
  Adjacent to the old store.

- **Flora Cemetery**
  1891.

- **Flora Store**
  Across from the livery.

Flora Church with Flora School behind

Flora to Enterprise

Distance:
35.9 miles

Directions:
From the Flora store, drive east on Flora Lane to the intersection of Flora Lane and Highway 3.

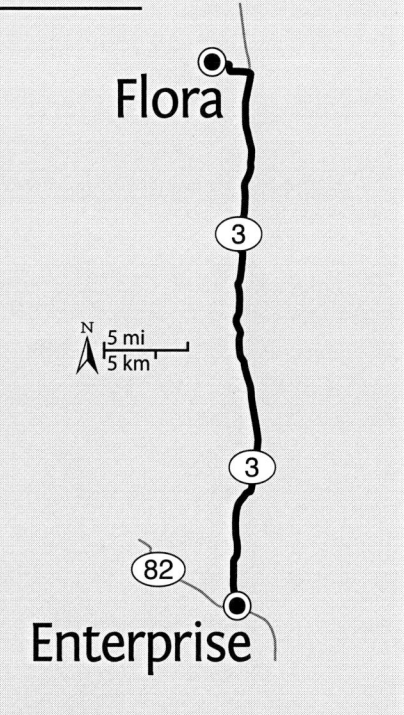

Points En Route

(mileage from the Flora store)

2.6 miles:
Intersection of Flora Lane and Highway 3. Turn right on Highway 3, returning south toward Enterprise.

30.5 miles:
Intersection of Highway 3 and Leap Lane. Stay on Highway 3.

32.8 miles:
Old barn.

34.9 miles:
Buffalo Ranch.

35.9 miles:
Enterprise

Enterprise

Elevation: 3757 feet

Location:
45.25.375 N • 117.17.853 W

Services: gas, food, lodging,

Enterprise is the largest community in Wallowa County and the commercial center of the broader Wallowa Valley basin. Wide-open, grassy meadows surround the town, with pine forests to the north and the scenic Wallowa Mountains to the south. Robert Stubblefield filed for the first homestead here in 1881 and, along with John Zurcher, platted the town in 1886. In 1887, under a tent owned by the local mercantile, several local residents assembled for the purpose of naming their city. Options included Bennett Flat, Wallowa City, Franklin and Fairfield. The name Enterprise was suggested by Stubblefield and received the majority of votes. The post office opened in 1887. Enterprise became the county seat in 1888 and was incorporated in 1889. Clydesdale draft horses used to be raised on a farm located between mileposts 66 and 67 on Highway 82.

Gotter Hotel

Points of Interest

- **First National Bank** (*10 Main*)
  Built in 1888.

- **Litch Building** (*100 Main*)
  Opened in 1909.

- **Enterprise Library**
  (*Main and 1st*)
  A Carnegie grant in 1913 helped to fund the construction of this library.

- **Enterprise Hotel** (*101 Main*)
  The hotel cost $10,000 to build in 1903. The third floor burned in 1936.

- **Bowlby Building** (*107 Main*)
  Built of Bowlby Stone in 1899 and housed the first drug store. The Masons were the initial second floor tenants.

- **Wallowa National Bank**
  (*121 Main*)
  Opened in 1885.

- **Christian Church**
  (*Main and 2nd*)
  The church was first chartered in 1893 and the building constructed in 1898. The parsonage was built later, in 1909.

- **Wallowa County Courthouse**
  (*207 Main*)
  Built in 1909 of Bowlby Stone.

- **Gotter Hotel** (*301 Main*)
  Built in 1918 and the last major commercial building constructed before 1941.

Walker House

- **Wallowa Chieftain** *(106 1st)*
  The new building was constructed in 1915, housing the 1884 newspaper.

- **IOOF Hall** *(1st and North)*
  Built in 1906.

- **Hyatt House** *(200 Greenwood)*
  Hyatt, president of the Enterprise Mercantile and Milling Company, built this house in 1898.

- **Ault House** *(301 Logan)*
  Circa 1905. One of the town's first doctors lived and practiced in this residence.

- **House** *(300 River)*
  The Craftsman was built in 1910 by the local druggist. It was a boarding house for local teachers and businesswomen.

- **Jordan House** *(101 3rd)*
  Queen Anne-style, built in 1900. Jordan's son became governor of Idaho.

- **Walker House** *(107 3rd)*
  This farmhouse was built in 1880 with an addition in 1920.

- **Enterprise Cemetery** *(4th)*
  Dates to the 1880s.

- **Warnock House** *(501 SE 5th)*
  Built in 1910.

Wallowa County Courthouse

Enterprise to Joseph

Distance:
7.7 miles

Directions:
At the intersection of 1st and North (Highway 82), stay on Highway 82 toward Joseph.

Points En Route

(mileage from 1st and North/Highway 82)

0.4 miles:
Turn right onto Hurricane Road.

3.5 miles:
Great view of the Wallowa Mountains.

4.9 miles:
Victorian house.

5.5 miles:
Stay left.

5.6 miles:
Hurricane Creek Grange.

6.6 miles:
Hurricane Creek Cemetery.

7.5 miles:
Chief Joseph Days Rodeo Grounds.

7.7 miles:
Joseph

Joseph

Elevation: 4191 feet

Location:
45.21.356 N • 117.13.789 W

Services: gas, food, lodging, B&B, RV, camping

Joseph is a lively, blossoming hub of the arts located near the foot of Wallowa Lake. The community was called both Silver Lake and Lake City, but duplication and name similarity led to the change in honor of the famous Nez Perce chief, Joseph. The post office opened in 1880, the local paper began publishing in 1883 and the city incorporated in 1887. Joseph became the county seat when Wallowa County separated from Union County in 1887, only to lose the distinction to Enterprise in 1888. The railroad reached town in 1908 and by 1920, Joseph bustled with a mercantile, doctor, dentist, electric company, lawyers, flour and sawmills, and hotels. Most of the buildings on Main Street are made of brick manufactured from local materials, mined from a deposit near the old schoolhouse. Walk on Main Street today, and discover a number of art galleries and antique stores. History buffs will enjoy the Wallowa County Museum and its interesting displays of pioneer life and the Nez Perce Tribe. Joseph is the gateway to Wallowa Lake, a recreational haven that, while at 5000 feet in elevation, is the largest body of water in Eastern Oregon.

Wallowa County Stage Stop

Points of Interest

- **Jennings Hotel** *(McCully and Main)*
  The 1906 hotel was made of locally manufactured brick and was the stage stop.

- **Dr. Barnard Drug Store** *(012 Main)*
  Barnard had a similar store in Enterprise. His name is inscribed in stone caps above the door.

- **Schleur Building** *(018 Main)*
  Originally a bar with upstairs hotel rooms. The large bar mirror and counter remain in the art gallery showroom.

- **First National Bank of Joseph** *(110 Main)*
  Built in 1888 of local brick and was Wallowa County's first bank. F.D. McCully was the president of the bank that was used as the hospital from 1913-1920. Allegedly, the bank was robbed and the convicted gunman became the bank president.

- **First National Bank Building** *(On Main between 1st and 2nd)*
  Stone caps display the name and 1908 date.

- **City Hall** *(201 Main)*
  Built in 1887.

Historic RR Depot

- **Converted Barn**
  (S East and E 3rd)
  A unique conversion to a family home.

- **Gaulke House** *(S Lake and E 3rd)*
  Built in the early 1900s, and home of the president of the First Bank of Joseph. The original wrought iron fence is intact.

- **Arthur Rudd House**
  (4th and Main)
  Built in 1910. The two front doors were built so that Rudd had entrances to both his home and business.

- **McKinley House** *(504 Main)*
  1909 Queen Anne Revival-style. The carriage house is now the garage.

- **Beith House** *(600 Main)*
  Built in 1905. Beith owned and operated the mercantile.

- **Rumble House** *(601 Main)*
  Another Craftsman-style home, built in the early 1900s.

- **Nusser House** *(101 S Mill)*
  Circa 1910, with a unique entrance.

- **Frank McCully House**
  (111 S Mill)
  Frank was instrumental in founding and incorporating the town. The home burned in 1915 and was rebuilt in 1918.

- **Fred McCully House**
  (201 S Mill)
  Queen Anne-Style, circa 1900. Built by the mercantile storeowner. Brother to Frank.

- **Eagles Haven B&B** *(208 S East)*
  Built in 1901 and converted to a B&B.

- **Chief Joseph Monument**
  (1.3 miles south of town)
  The 1927 burial site of the famous Nez Perce leader.

- **Wallowa Lake**
  (4.5 miles south of town)
  Camping, RV, groceries, state park, lodges, fishing, swimming and boat launch. The lake was formed by a series of glacial scouring. Look for lateral and terminal moraine around the rim of the lake. The Mt. Howard Tram operates here and offers breathtaking views of the Eagle Cap Wilderness.

- **Eagle Cap Excursion Train**
  Passes through the rugged canyons of the Wallowa Valley.

Eagles Haven B&B

First National Bank Building

Rudd House

First National Bank of Joseph

Joseph to Imnaha

Distance:
29.5 miles

Directions:
At the intersection of Main and Wallowa, go north on Wallowa. Wallowa will turn into Little Sheep Creek Road and is the Hell's Canyon Scenic By-Way.

Points En Route

(mileage from the intersection of Main and Wallowa)

2.0 miles:
Joseph Cemetery Road. The cemetery dates to the late 1890s.

2.1 miles:
A frequently photographed, red barn. The barn was owned by movie actor and TV star Walter Brennan.

5.5 miles:
Winter Ski area. Continue on Little Sheep Creek Road.

6.4 miles:
This begins a 23.1-mile downgrade.

8.1 miles:
Junction with Wallowa Mountain Road. Continue straight on Little Sheep Creek Road.

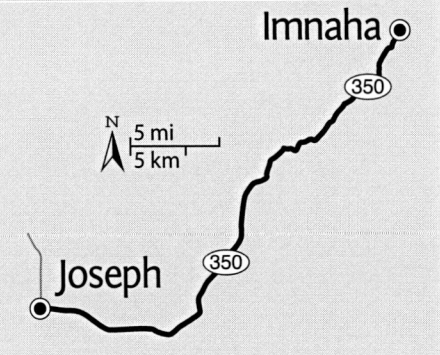

10.2 miles:
Picturesque, old barn.

20.2 miles:
M and M Ranch.

21.0 miles:
Hells Canyon Kiosk.

21.3 miles:
Devils Gulch, hiking trails and natural area.

21.5 miles:
Little Sheep Wildlife Area.

25.4 miles:
Old, abandoned homestead.

29.4 miles:
Imnaha School.

29.5 miles:
Imnaha

Imnaha

Elevation: 2091 feet

Location:
45.33.500 N • 116.50.011 W

Services: food, B&B

Lewis and Clark called this area Imnahar. The post office opened in 1887 and the town was established by 1901. A general store and church were the first buildings in the new community. Imnaha hosts a 'Rattlesnake and Bear feed' every year.

Points of Interest:

- **Imnaha Store and Tavern**
  Operating since 1904. A freezer chest, located inside, is full of rattlesnakes killed by local residents for the annual feed.

- **Hells Canyon Roadhouse**
  Circa 1905.

- **Imnaha Post Office**
  The Zip Code is 97842 and the building is about 100 years old.

- **Historic Marker**
  Located next to the store and tavern.

Imnaha Store and Tavern

Hells Canyon Roadhouse

Imnaha Post Office

Alternate Return to Joseph

The Upper Imnaha River Road is a 65.8-mile alternate return route to Joseph. The 30.5-mile, graveled road follows the Imnaha River. Features of this alternate route include beautiful scenery and more. At mile 14.6 is an old schoolhouse. The Imnaha River Woods Subdivision is located at mile 22.8. At 25.9 miles is a survivalist ranch built by movie star Eugene Palette in the 1930s. A fish weir is located at 29.3 miles. The remainder of the drive is paved and includes a breathtaking overlook of Little Sheep Creek at 37.6 miles.

Notes